Communities

KEYWORDS IN TEACHER EDUCATION

SERIES EDITOR: VIV ELLIS

Taking cultural theorist Raymond Williams's concept as an organizing device, the **Keywords in Teacher Education** series offers short, accessibly written books on the most pressing and challenging ideas in the field.

Teacher education has a high profile in public policy and professional debates given the enduring associations between how teachers are prepared and how well their students do in school. At the same time, research perspectives on the important topics in the field are increasingly polarized with important consequences for the kind of teacher and the qualities of teaching that are most valued. Written by internationally recognized experts, these titles offer analyses both of the historical emergence and the consequences of the different positions in these debates.

ALSO AVAILABLE IN THE SERIES:

Expertise, Jessica Gerrard and Jessica Holloway
Identity, Sarah Steadman
Quality, Clare Brooks

FORTHCOMING IN THE SERIES:

Disadvantage, Jo Lampert, Jane Wilkinson, Mervi Kaukko and Rocío García-Carrión
Knowledge, Steven Puttick, Victoria Elliott and Jenni Ingram

Communities

KENNETH M. ZEICHNER

BLOOMSBURY ACADEMIC
LONDON • NEW YORK • OXFORD • NEW DELHI • SYDNEY

BLOOMSBURY ACADEMIC
Bloomsbury Publishing Plc
50 Bedford Square, London, WC1B 3DP, UK
1385 Broadway, New York, NY 10018, USA
29 Earlsfort Terrace, Dublin 2, Ireland

BLOOMSBURY, BLOOMSBURY ACADEMIC and the Diana logo are
trademarks of Bloomsbury Publishing Plc

First published in Great Britain 2024

Cover design by Charlotte James
Cover image © Zoonar GmbH / Alamy Stock Photo

A catalogue record for this book is available from the British Library.

A catalog record for this book is available from the Library of Congress.

ISBN: HB: 978-1-3501-7334-7
PB: 978-1-3501-7333-0
ePDF: 978-1-3501-7336-1
eBook: 978-1-3501-7335-4

Series: Keywords in Teacher Education

Typeset by Deanta Global Publishing Services, Chennai, India

To find out more about our authors and books visit www.bloomsbury.com
and sign up for our newsletters.

To Andrea

CONTENTS

List of Figure viii
Series Editor's Foreword ix
Preface xiii
Acknowledgments xxi

1 Why Should We Care About Communities in Teacher Education? 1
2 An Overview of the Trajectory of Communities in US Teacher Education 19
3 Various Interpretations of Communities in Teacher Education 41
4 Creating the Conditions in Teacher Education Programs for Preparing Community-Focused Culturally Responsive and Sustaining Teachers 73

Notes 101
References 105
Index 125

FIGURE

3.1 Community participation in teacher education 42

SERIES EDITOR'S FOREWORD

This series is organized by the concept of "keywords," first elaborated by Welsh cultural theorist Raymond Williams (1976), and books in the series will seek to problematize and unsettle the ostensibly unproblematic and settled vocabulary of teacher education. From Williams' perspective, keywords are words and phrases that occur frequently in speech and writing, allowing conversation to ensue, but that nonetheless reveal profound differences in meaning within and across cultures, politics, and histories. In teacher education, such keywords include practice, knowledge, quality, and expertise. The analysis of such keywords allows us to trace the evolution of the emergent—and the maintenance of residual—meanings in teacher education discourses and practices. By analyzing keywords, therefore, it is possible to elucidate the range of meanings of what Gallie (1955) referred to as "essentially contested concepts" but in ways that promote a critical, historical understanding of changes in the fields in which they occur.

In the first edition of *Keywords*, Williams included entries on 108 units, ranging from "Aesthetic" to "Work." A second edition followed in 1983 and other writers have subsequently used the concept to expand on Williams' original collection (e.g., Bennett et al., 2005; MacCabe & Yanacek, 2018) or to apply the concept to specific domains (e.g., A Community of Inquiry, 2018). This series applies it to teacher education. The purpose of the series mirrors that of Williams' original project: to trace ideological differences and social conflicts over time as they relate to the discourses and practices of a field (here, teacher education) by focusing on a selection of the field's high-frequency words. So *Keywords in Teacher Education* is not a multivolume dictionary.

The kind of analysis required by a focus on keywords goes beyond etymology or historical semantics. By selecting and analyzing keywords, Williams argued:

> we find a history and complexity of meanings; conscious changes, or consciously different uses; innovation, obsolescence, specialization, extension, overlap, transfer; or changes which are masked by a nominal continuity so that words which seem to have been there for centuries, with continuous general meanings, have come in fact to express radically different or radically variable, yet sometimes hardly noticed, meanings and implications of meaning. (Williams, 1976, p. 17)

Given the increasingly strong attention paid to teacher education in education policy and in public debates about education more generally, focusing on keywords in this field is both timely and necessary. Uncovering and unsettling differences and conflicts in the vocabulary of preparing teachers render the political and social bases underlying policy formation and public discourse more visible and therefore more capable of being acted upon.

Through this organizing device, the *Keywords in Teacher Education* series addresses the most important topics and questions in teacher education currently. It is a series of short books written in a direct and accessible style, each book taking one keyword as its point of departure and closely examining its cultural meanings historically while, crucially, identifying the social forces and material consequences of the differences and conflicts in meaning. Written by internationally recognized researchers, each peer-reviewed book offers cutting-edge analysis of the keyword underpinned by a deep knowledge of the available research within the field—and beyond it. One of the aims of the series is to broaden the gaze of teacher education research by engaging more systematically with the relevant humanities and social science literature—to acknowledge, as Williams did, that our understanding is deepened and potential for action strengthened by seeking to understand the social relations between words, texts, and the multiple contexts in which their meanings are produced.

Community was one of Williams' original keywords from the book's first edition. Emphasizing the consistently seductive nature of its meanings, Williams wrote:

> *Community* can be the warmly persuasive word to describe an existing set of relationships, or the warmly persuasive word to describe an alternative set of relationships. What is most important, perhaps, is that unlike all other terms of social organisation (*state, nation, society,* etc.), it seems never to be used unfavourably, and never to be given any positive opposing or distinguishing term. (Williams, 1976, p. 66)

In this personally reflective and critical contribution to the series, Ken Zeichner focuses intensely on the meanings of *communities* (plural) and the evolution of these meanings in the field of teacher education. These meanings have been shaped by the interactions of the discourses of teacher education with other discourses from related fields, including politics (with its sense of "grass roots" activism) and psychology (with its interest in human development through "communities of practice"), among others. Who and what is a community? What are and what should be the relationships between communities? To what extent does a phrase like "community-engaged" represent a more democratic and democratizing, institutionalized form of teacher preparation? What makes the use of community always and everywhere so "warmly persuasive"—and what contradictions does this warm persuasion obscure?

Zeichner directly addresses these questions and others in a book that encapsulates his long-standing and distinctive interests in the relationships between a specialized field of activity like teacher education and wider societal priorities such as equity and social justice. It is in addressing these societal priorities that Zeichner demonstrates why what communities mean—the clarity of its definitions—is so important.

Viv Ellis
Melbourne, 2023

References

A Community of Inquiry. (2018). *Keywords; for further consideration and particularly relevant to academic life, especially as it concerns disciplines, inter-disciplinary endeavor and modes of resistance to the same*. Princeton, NJ: Princeton University Press.

Bennett, T., Grossberg, L., & Morris, M. (2005). *New keywords. A revised vocabulary of culture and society*. Oxford: Blackwell Publishing.

Ericsson, K. A., Krampe, R. T., & Tesch-Romer, C. (1993). The role of deliberate practice in the acquisition of expert performance. *Psychological Review, 100*(3), 363–406.

Gallie, W. B. (1955). Essentially contested concepts. *Proceedings of the Aristotelian Society, 56*, 167–198.

McCabe, C., Yanacek, H., & the Keywords Project. (2018). *Keywords for today. A 21st century vocabulary*. Oxford: Oxford University Press.

Williams, R. (1976). *Keywords: A vocabulary of culture and society*. London: Fontana.

PREFACE

The term "communities" is an ambiguous concept that has many different meanings within and across academic disciplines and in everyday discourse (Delanty, 2018; MacCabe & Yanacek, 2018; Williams, 1976). This book is about the various meanings that the concept of communities has taken on over time within the field of teacher education, both within the United States and internationally. In teacher education, communities have been used in relation to the nature and quality of the relationships among teacher educators or teacher candidates within a program and between teacher educators and the educators and others who live in the local geographical areas in which they prepare teachers.

Here I will focus on the ways in which community members who are external to teacher preparation programs (students' families and others who live in the areas near the schools where teacher candidates learn to teach) have participated in the education of teachers. I will also focus on the ways in which teacher candidates learn about the families of their students and the communities in which they live, and what they do with this knowledge as teachers. Finally, this book focuses on a particular subset of communities that has been a focus in the work of many teacher education programs around the world. I will introduce this more specific community context through a discussion of my own formative experiences as a public school teacher and teacher educator and of how central my work in and with communities was to my development as an educator.

In July 1969, following my graduation from Temple University in Philadelphia with a degree in pre-law and a week or so before the Apollo 11 landing on the moon, I began a one-year master's degree program at Syracuse University ("The Urban Teacher Preparation Program") to earn my teaching certification in grades one through six. This program focused on preparing teachers for "Title I" schools[1] whose mission was to serve nondominant communities highly impacted by poverty.

In part, because my own high school experience in Philadelphia Public Schools enabled me to see and experience first-hand the impact of inequitable education opportunities (Kitzmiller, 2022), I wanted to teach in urban schools that I believed could help me contribute to the kind of broad social transformation that was being sought by many in the United States at that time. The unpopular war in Vietnam and mandatory racial segregation and voter suppression laws intended to violate the constitutional rights of African Americans were being protested on a large scale. The groundbreaking Civil Rights and Voting Rights Acts had become law across the nation just a few years before, and in cities all over the country communities highly impacted by poverty and lacking meaningful influence on their neighborhood schools were seeking to gain more authentic voice and influence in their local public schools in the midst of a broad effort in many nondominant communities to act back against the racism, discrimination, and exclusion that had affected all aspects of community life.

In late summer, after completing a few courses, including a sociology course on urban communities, and a practicum in a summer school, I was assigned for my nine-month internship to an elementary school that had recently made major changes in an attempt to become more responsive to the predominately low-income and African American families it was supposed to serve in its mostly racially segregated neighborhood. From my first day as an intern teacher,[2] I learned that the students, their families, and the broader community whom we were supposed to serve were at the center of the work of our school. The new African American principal who had been hired shortly before I had arrived at the school implemented a new school governance model that established a school cabinet composed of a few teachers, students' family members, other community members, and the principal. The cabinet deliberated about the use of resources in the school, participated in the hiring and evaluation of staff, and generally worked to make the school a more helpful resource for the whole community rather than serving as a fortress within the community as had been true for this school and for so many other schools in US urban neighborhoods at that time (Cuban, 1969).

During my seven years at the school, a community liaison was hired and courses were developed and offered at night and on the weekends by community and school instructors for adults and youth. The course topics were chosen on the basis of community preference. In addition to community members on the school cabinet, several local parents and community members worked in the school as teacher assistants and lunchroom aides. There was a big sign in the hallway near the front entrance to the school that said something like "This is a community school. All are welcome." Our school received grant funding from the Mott Foundation to support its conversion to a public community school to serve as a resource to the entire community (Oakes, Maier, & Daniel, 2017).

As a new teacher, I learned that my role as a teacher was not just with my students, but to also contribute to the welfare of the broader community. This message was in contradiction to the dominant messages in teacher education programs at that time about high-poverty communities of "cultural deprivation" and the need to try to rescue students from their allegedly broken communities (Reissman, 1962).

All teachers in our school were required by our principal to visit the families of all of their students before the school year began to begin to establish trusting relationships with them, and we were encouraged to spend time in the community shopping, attending community events, getting to know the people and resources in the community, and learning how to utilize community resources and the cultural wealth in the community in our teaching. I taught grades four, five, and six at this school for seven years which was my entire public school teaching experience. My life as a public school teacher included a natural extension of my classroom work into the surrounding community. At times, there were conflicts among the staff and between staff and community members, both those who worked in the school and those who did not. The work of school-community collaboration was not always easy, but the relationships of trust that emerged over time between school and community members made this work worthwhile, enhanced the quality and relevance of our teaching, and helped build greater community trust in their neighborhood school.

After a few years, I remained at the school and began my first job as a teacher educator with the Teacher Corps (TC). TC was a federal program that existed in 75–100 urban and rural communities highly impacted by poverty and was designed to prepare teachers to be successful in their Title 1 schools and remain there over time (Edelfelt, Corwin, & Hanna, 1974). The TC was founded on the idea that communities highly impacted by poverty that for many years generally lacked voice and influence in the schools that were supposed to educate their children should be central contributors to the education of their children in public schools and to the education of the teachers who worked there.

Each TC project was governed by a local board and steering committee that had an equal number of university, school, and community members. TC interns in this two-year initial certification program were required to spend about 25 percent of their time working collaboratively with community members on projects that benefited the broader community and that community members led (Masla & Royster, 1976). My role as a mentor and supervisor for a team of five TC interns during their two-year internship was to supervise and support both their work in the classroom and in the broader community. Thus, in my upbringing as both a teacher and teacher educator, I learned the value and importance of community voice and expertise in supporting the success of public schools in communities highly impacted by poverty and the many "rotten outcomes" that are associated with poverty (Schorr, 1988).

My experiences in learning to be a teacher and teacher educator are in sharp contrast to the experiences of most teachers, teacher candidates, and teacher educators then and now in the United States and internationally. Although there has been much rhetoric about the importance of the role of families and communities in schools and teacher preparation programs for over seventy years (e.g., Flowers et al., 1948), in reality in the United States and in many other parts of the world, there has been very little attention to the issue of preparing teachers to work with families and communities, especially in communities highly impacted by poverty (e.g., deBrune et al., 2014; Epstein & Sanders, 2006; Thompson et al., 2018). Furthermore, even when such attention has been present in teacher education programs, it has most often employed university and/or school-centric rather than family and community-centric forms of collaboration, especially in relation to families and communities highly impacted by poverty (Baquedano-Lopez, Alexander, & Hernandez, 2013). These school/university-centric approaches often reflect deficit views of families and communities highly impacted by poverty and position families and communities in ways where they are expected to conform to the ways of the school while they neglect the potential value of the schools learning from the families and communities (Ishimaru, 2019; Schutz, 2006). In addition, although there has been much rhetoric about the importance of community engagement in teacher education programs, teacher educators have rarely modeled the community engagement practices that they advocate for teacher candidates to use in schools thereby undermining any words they might speak about the importance of engaging families and communities. As Cuban (1969) asserts:

When professors talk about the importance of getting involved in the community and knowing its dynamics, yet members of the community are rarely seen on campus and students only take occasional field trips . . . there is an inconsistency. . . . Action and behavior carry far more weight than words. (p. 260, 261)

This book discusses the various ways in which families and communities have connected to initial teacher education programs in the United States and internationally. The specific focus is on families and communities that have been historically marginalized and are highly impacted by poverty. While it is important for all families and communities to have an authentic and influential voice in the education of their children and the education of the teachers who teach their children, it is families and communities that have been highly impacted by poverty and that have been historically marginalized who typically lack voice and influence in their community's schools.

> Voicelessness and a general lack of participation sum up the inner-city community's role in the affairs of the school. (Cuban, 1969, p. 253)[3]

I use the term "nondominant families and communities" to indicate my focus on this particular set of families and communities. Ishimaru et al. (2019) define nondominant families and communities as

> Those impacted by systematic oppression such as marginalization based on race, class, language or immigration status. (p. 9)

In this book, I attempt to clarify the various meanings of communities in teacher education in the United States and internationally rather than provide a comprehensive review of the research on communities and teacher education. Chapter 1 discusses the importance of school-community connections in nondominant communities and what is known about the nature and quality of these relationships and their potential benefits for student learning and development. It also discusses what we know from research about the importance of strong school-family and community relations to the education of teacher candidates who teach students from nondominant communities and of the importance of preparing teachers to teach in culturally responsive and sustaining ways to the success of students in these schools.

Chapter 2 begins with a broad overview of the development of communities in teacher education in the United States in the last seventy-five years. I use this historical overview to develop a typology that identifies some of the critical dimensions of variation in concepts and practices among different instances of communities in teacher education This typology has three main dimensions: (1) the participation of community members in teacher education programs; (2) community experiences for teacher candidates in their programs; and (3) the recruitment and preparation of people from nondominant communities to teach in these communities.

In Chapter 3, I discuss a set of design principles for community-centered work in TPPs that are suggested by existing research. In doing so, I seek to illuminate the kinds of conditions that teacher educators should seek to establish in the three areas addressed by the framework presented in Chapter 2: community participation in teacher preparation programs, teacher candidate experiences in communities, and preparing homegrown teachers in nondominant communities.

In Chapter 4, I summarize the program design conditions that were introduced in Chapter 3, and I then discuss some of the structural, resource, and policy issues related to teacher preparation programs being able to support and sustain community engagement as a fundamental part of the work they do over time. In this chapter, I also discuss the question of whether university-based teacher education or school-district-based teacher education programs potentially have the capacity to genuinely engage with communities in their work under conditions of mutual benefit and mutual respect or whether new structures need to be created to make this kind of shared responsibility for teacher preparation more common and sustainable over time.

Finally, when I use the term "teacher education program" in this book, I am referring to all of the different forms of teacher education that have emerged internationally in recent decades. Although in the United States and other OECD member countries, college or university-based teacher education continues to be the dominant form of teacher preparation, teacher preparation programs that exist outside of colleges and universities have become more common in many parts of the world including in some OECD countries such as the United Kingdom and United States. I will argue that most of the traditional and newer forms of initial teacher education that currently exist have largely neglected the role of families and communities in the education of teachers for nondominant communities including some of the new more hybrid programs like teacher residency programs that involve partnerships between schools and university or non-university programs. The exceptions to this conclusion are community-based Grow Your Own (GYO) programs and Indigenous teacher education programs that are discussed in Chapter 2, where the community or tribal perspectives are often at the center of everything that is done in the programs.

ACKNOWLEDGMENTS

I would like to thank the following people who contributed to my writing of this book either by reading earlier drafts of chapters and giving me helpful feedback, sending me information in response to my requests, teaching me important lessons about how to become a better collaborator with communities in preparing teachers, or some combination of the above. I would also like to thank the three anonymous reviewers of my draft manuscript and Viv Ellis, the editor of this book series, who provided me with specific and thoughtful feedback and suggestions.

Lynne Boyle-Baise, Megan Bang, Meghan Barnes, Dawn Bennett, Marisa Bier, Anthony Craig, Gloria Ladson-Billings, Michael Bowman, Margaret Caspe, Andreal and Arlington Davis, Chinh Nguyen Duc, Jolyn Gardner, Lauren Gatti, Jenny Gawronski, Geneva Gay, Maureen Gillette, Amaya Gomez, Lin Goodwin, Margery Ginsberg, Carl Grant, Rita Green, Lorena Guillen, Demetria Iazzetto, Ann Ishimaru, David and Scott Imig, Mary Klehr, Rita Kohli, Kerry Kretchmar, Jo Lampert, Robert Lee, Ethan Loewenstein, Filiberto Barajas-Lopez, Susan Melnick, Lucy Mule, Peter Murrell, Noshini Naidoo, Jennifer O'Malley, Nadine Peterson, Kate Napolitan, Paul Ontooguk, Katie Payne, Thomas Phillip, Christine Sleeter, Dawn Hardison-Stevens, Kerry Cooley-Stroum, Beth West, and Eva Zygmunt.

CHAPTER ONE

Why Should We Care About Communities in Teacher Education?

Teachers simply do not teach effectively when they hold inaccurate deficit views of children, families, and communities. Nor can they scaffold their instruction on what students already know if they do not acknowledge the skills and capabilities that children bring with them. (Schultz, 2006, p. 726)

As stated in the Preface, the term "community" in relation to schools refers in this book to the families and neighborhoods in which students in particular schools live. In the context of teacher education programs, community refers to the families and neighborhoods served by the schools in which clinical placements are made and to a lesser extent to the broader local contexts (town, city, county) in which these schools are located.

Parts of this chapter are based on a talk presented at the 2021 annual meeting of the Australian Association for Teacher Education, a summary of which has been published as. Zeichner, K. (2022). Interview with Ken Zeichner: Current challenges and future possibilities for teacher education. *Asia-Pacific Journal of Teacher Education*, 50(2), 130–43.

These definitions are consistent with William's (1976) depiction of community as something more immediate than society, "the common people, as distinguished from those of rank" (p. 39).

Also, as mentioned previously, the focus in this book is on "nondominant communities" that have been historically marginalized and oppressed by formal systems. Ishimaru et al. (2019) define nondominant families and communities as

> Those impacted by systemic oppression such as marginalization based on race, class, language, or immigration status. (p. 9)

These are the communities as Barajas-Lopez and Ishimaru (2020) point out that in the US experience many "challenges of health care, housing, immigration, transportation, and other underlying dynamics facing schools" (p. 39). Finally, these are also the communities that suffer from an inequitable distribution of resources such as public education funding per pupil and an inequitable share of fully prepared experienced teachers teaching in their areas of certification (Baker, 2018; Darling-Hammond, 2013).

In the United States, the majority of students who attend public schools live in poverty as measured by their qualified status for the federal free or reduced meal program. In the fall of 2019, 52.3 percent of pupils were in this category (Hogdon & Saunders, 1951). In some parts of the country, the percentage of students living in poverty in 2019 was even greater (e.g., District of Columbia, 76.4 percent; Mississippi, 76.4 percent) (National Center for Education Statistics 2021, 2022). Additionally, BIPOC[1] students who attend US public schools, who made up 54.2 percent of the public school students in 2020,[2] are concentrated in high-poverty schools in nondominant communities. The US government defines high-poverty schools as those where more than 75 percent of the students are eligible for free or reduced-price lunch under the National School Lunch Program. A concentration of BIPOC students in high-poverty schools is shown in fall

2019 data published by the National Center for Education Statistics: 45 percent of Black students, 43 percent of Hispanic students, 37 percent of Native American Indian/Alaska Native students, 25 percent of Pacific Islander students, 17 percent of mixed-race students, 14 percent of Asian students, while only 8 percent of White students attend high-poverty schools (National Center for Education Statistics, 2022).

Although the issues that are discussed in this book apply to all types of families and communities in different ways, the focus here is limited to schools in nondominant communities and the urgency of addressing the long-standing disconnects and the lack of community voice and influence in schools and teacher education programs. There are also problems of course between families and communities, schools, and teacher education programs in more elite communities. Although there is some overlap between the issues in these contexts, the problems and the strategies for addressing the tensions between schools and elite communities are very different than those that will be discussed in this book given the vast power differences that commonly exist between elite and nondominant communities with regard to schools (e.g., Baquedano et al., 2013; Lareau, 2000).

Currently, there are communities across the United States where primarily White parents are demanding that their public schools stop teaching students about the historical and systemic racism within the society (e.g., in access to housing, voting rights, transportation, and in the criminal justice system) that has defined the United States since its beginnings. There also have been attempts in some of these communities to ban teaching in schools about US civil rights struggles,[3] the discussion of LGBGT issues,[4] as well as the use of certain words and books, and educators have been disciplined in some school districts and terminated in others[5] for allegedly disregarding these bans. In some cases, states are trying to require teachers to post their plans and materials online several days before using them so that parents can raise objections to what will be taught.[6] My focus here is on the long-standing tensions between public schools and nondominant immigrant communities and communities of color that have historically lacked voice and power in influencing the education that their children receive in public schools (Cuban, 1969) in the United States and internationally (Grace, 2006).

The motives of families and community members in nondominant communities to fight for schools and teacher preparation programs to embrace the funds of knowledge and cultural wealth in their communities to enhance the education of their children are democratic ones. Their goals are to help provide more equitable educational opportunities for their children, an education in which all students feel valued and affirmed in school. On the other hand, the motives of families and community members who are working to suppress the teaching of an accurate history of racism and other forms of discrimination in their public schools are exclusionary ones that clearly undermine fundamental democratic principles that protect the rights of all citizens to be treated equitably (Guttman, 1999). Some among those who are currently pushing for imposing their own personal and/or religious beliefs on everyone want to end public schooling entirely and shift the government funds that now support public schools to private and religious schools (Schneider & Berkshire, 2020).

To support greater responsiveness by public/state schools to nondominant communities is not to call for families and community members to be able to dictate to educators about what should be taught in schools and how it should be taught. Increasing the voice and influence of community members on the education of their children in public/state schools does not mean that educators should blindly follow what the most vocal members of a community want them to do. On the contrary, what is involved here is the shift to a form of professionalism for educators in which educators and teacher educators, and community members work in genuinely collaborative ways to connect education and teacher education to the needs and goals of particular nondominant communities. Sachs (2001) has argued that this "democratic professionalism":

Seeks to demystify professional work and build alliances between teachers and excluded constituencies of students, parents, and members of the community on whose behalf decisions have traditionally been made either by professionals or by the state . . . the core of democratic professionalism is an emphasis on collaborative cooperative action between teachers and other education stakeholders. (p. 153)

In many nondominant communities in the United States and elsewhere, organized efforts by community members to address systemic problems in housing, access to nutritious food, crime, transportation, access to affordable childcare, access to a living wage, and access to an equitable education have existed for many years (e.g., Anyon, 2014; Warren & Goodman, 2018). Democratic professionalism in education centers students, families, and communities in teachers' work and in educating teachers and joins the work of education in democratic societies to existing organized struggles in nondominant communities for a more equitable share of a society's resources (Zeichner, 2019a).

Although I have only quoted statistics here from the United States on the segregation of pupils from nondominant communities in public schools, nondominant communities and the segregation of students in publicly or state-run schools by race and social class also exist in many other countries. Throughout the world, whether families in nondominant communities send their children to private schools, religious schools, tribal schools, or public/state schools, these children almost always attend schools that receive fewer resources and have teachers that are less experienced than the ones attended by children from elite communities. The nondominant communities are the ones where there are many teachers who were prepared to teach on the job while they were full-time teachers and where there is a shortage of experienced teachers because of high teacher turnover. Examples of this problem internationally can be found in the communities in the sixty-one countries where the program *Teach for All* sends underprepared teachers to teach "other people's children elsewhere for a while" (Ellis et al. 2016; Thomas, Raushenberger, & Crawford-Thomas, 2022).

Teaching in Nondominant Communities

In the United States and other countries that have experienced a growth in refugees and immigrants in their populations, teachers who work in nondominant communities in which many immigrants, refugees, and others who live in poverty are faced with a situation where they often bring very little personal experience to be able to draw on when trying to connect with their students and their families (Epstein & Sanders, 2006). Very often teachers do not live in or have much experience with the nondominant communities in which they teach, and very few of them have been prepared in their teacher education programs for how to work in mutually respectful ways with their students' families and to learn about the expertise and cultural wealth in their communities and how to connect their curriculum and classroom instruction with students' lives outside of the classroom (Hong, 2019). Neither are most teachers in schools in nondominant communities provided with ongoing professional learning opportunities and encouragement from their school administrators to support their efforts to engage families and learn about their communities (Kirmaci, 2019; Weiss, Lopez, & Caspe, 2018).

Disconnect and Distrust between Families, Communities, and Schools in Nondominant Communities

One consequence of the long-standing disconnect and the power differentials between nondominant communities and educators in the schools their children attend is the perpetuation of deficit views by educators about their students' families and the communities in which their students live and the absence of community cultures, languages, and practices in the schools attended by nondominant students. The absence of community cultural practices in many of these schools has had a negative impact on students' well-being and learning.

> When schools are not inclusive of the communities' languages, practices, and knowledge, they tend to alienate students and their families and thus put these students at continued risk for failure in dominant educational settings. (Philip et al. 2013, p. 175)

A view of social mobility and education with regard to nondominant communities has often been associated with deficit perspectives of families and community members based on the false idea that educational attainment for students in these communities requires them to be able to "escape" their communities for a better life somewhere else (Ishimaru et al., 2019). Despite good intentions, educators have often focused on changing or trying to "fix" marginalized parents and caregivers and to "save" students from their communities.

In order for teachers to be able to help disrupt the failure that has persisted in schools in nondominant communities, they need to be able to see their students not as isolated individuals but as members of families and communities, and to see and appreciate the funds of knowledge and cultural wealth that families and communities possess (Capatano & Huisman, 2010; Watson, 2012). Teachers must also learn to see the possibility that families and community members can help them do a better job in educating their children. Additionally, teachers must also learn to see themselves as part of the communities in which they work even though they may not live there (Ladson-Billings, 2021) and to view their work as contributing to helping these communities realize greater educational justice and community well-being in and outside of education.

One consequence of the long-standing lack of genuine voice of nondominant communities in their public schools is the existence of mutual distrust that exists among educators and families and community members. Bryk and Schneider's (2002) description of the tensions between schools and nondominant communities in Chicago over two decades ago still holds true today in many nondominant communities in the United States and internationally. Tensions between educators and communities continue to undermine the quality of learning for students in nondominant communities.

> Distrust now characterizes many of the social interactions that poor families have with local schools and other public institutions. Teachers often see parents' goals and values as impediments to students' academic accomplishments. Parents in turn, believe that teachers are antagonistic toward them and fail to appreciate the actual conditions that shape their children's lives. This lack of trust between teachers and parents—often exacerbated by race and class differences-makes it difficult for these groups to maintain a genuine dialogue about shared concerns. The resultant miscommunications tend to reinforce existing prejudices and undermine constructive efforts by teachers and parents to build relational ties around the interests of children. Instead of working together to support the academic and social development of students, teachers and parents find themselves working in isolation, or, in worst cases, in opposition to each one another. . . . Unless substantial attention focuses on strengthening the social relationships among school professionals and parents, efforts at instructional improvement are unlikely to succeed (pp. 6, 8).

Research on school improvement and policy efforts has consistently supported the conclusion that the authentic engagement of families and communities in schools from the very beginning and mutual trust between families and communities and educators are important features of improvement efforts that result in positive outcomes for students (Bryk & Schneider, 2002; Comer, Haynes, Joyner & Ben-Avie, 1996; Hong, 2019; Ishimaru, 2020). When these features are missing from school improvement efforts, educators, the state, or educational entrepreneurs try to push reforms through on their own with families and communities playing passive and symbolic roles, and the result has often been failure and maintenance of the status quo or worse (e.g., Ewing, 2018; Miner, 2013; Russakoff, 2015).

Research in the United States and internationally has shown that effective home-school relations (especially in nondominant communities) are important for students' well-being and academic learning. For example:

> Decades of research have focused on parents as key levers for improving children's educational success and parent and family involvement is consistently associated with positive educational outcomes for children. (Ishimaru, 2020, p. 15)

However, not any kind of family community participation with schools will necessarily lead to positive learning outcomes for students (Weiss, Lopez, & Rosenberg, 2010; Weiss, Lopez, & Caspe, 2018). Unfortunately, much of what has occurred in school-family and community relations in nondominant communities has framed parents and community members as lacking and in need of support or fixing rather than as assets who can help teachers do their jobs better. These experiences often reflect doubts by educators that parents and communities can be equal partners in educating a community's children (Baquedano-Lopez, Alexander, & Hernandez, 2013; Driscoll, 1998; Dryness, 2011; Ishimaru, 2020). What is absent from many, if not most, school-family and community interactions in nondominant communities is the recognition by educators that families and community members have expertise about their children and communities that can help educators do a better job of educating their children.

Families and communities possess vital knowledge and expertise not only about their own individual children, but also about their communities, their histories and systemic educational inequities in and out of schools. Such knowledge and expertise are not simply assets to appreciate. They are vital building blocks for efforts to transform our schools and broader systems toward educational justice. (Ishimaru et al., 2019, p. 12)

Involving versus Engaging Families and Communities in Schools

Educators say they value parent participation, but they often mean a junior partner role in which parents monitor homework, make sure kids get to school on time, show up at school sponsored events and generally act as an extension of the teacher and the school. Many parents and community advocates see themselves as more than just a supporting cast. (Gold, Henig, & Simon, 2011, p. 34)

There is widespread consensus in scholarship on family/community-school relations that there are two major types of family and community participation in schools: involvement and engagement. Waller (1932), in his classic text on the sociology of teaching, identified the ways in which schools most often seek to involve parents and community members in school-centric ways.

Parent-teacher work has usually been directed at securing for the school the support of parents, that is, getting parents to see children more or less as teachers see them. But it would be a sad day for childhood if parent-teacher work ever really succeeded in its object. (p. 69)[7]

Much of the effort that has been made by schools in nondominant communities to encourage family and community *involvement* has been done in ways where the roles of parents and community members are severely restricted and reactive, and limited to responding to things that have already been framed by educators (Baquedano-Lopez, Alexander, & Hernandez, 2013; Calabrese-Barton, Drake, Perez, St. Louis, & George, 2004; Ishimaru, 2020). Usually, educators want families to listen and react to what they have to say about their children, about what the school thinks that they can do at home to enhance their children's education, or to contribute time to raising money to support school programs.

The school-centric focus in these efforts is frequently on getting families to comply with the wishes of the school and to volunteer time to help the school carry out its agenda. Generally, there has been very little interest in finding out and discussing what issues nondominant families and community members want to discuss or in learning about and taking advantage of the expertise and cultural wealth (Yosso, 2005) that exists in nondominant families and communities (e.g., Watson, 2012).[8]

> Conventional approaches to engaging nondominant parents in education for example, attendance at school open houses, parent-teacher conferences, and parent-teacher association meetings-are rooted in conceptions of parents and families as deficient, sometimes lacking in knowledge, skills, capital, and capacities, and at other times as lacking more fundamentally in caring or will. (Barajas-Lopez & Ishimaru, 2020, p. 39)

In the last two decades, there has been a growth of educators and scholars who have explicitly rejected the school-centered and compliance-oriented approach connected to community involvement and have called for community *engagement,* which potentially implies a more active and equitable role for families and community members in schools in nondominant communities. Although the shift in emphasis from involvement to engagement in both scholarship and practice has made more visible the deficiencies of an involvement approach and has provided more opportunities in some circumstances for families and community members to participate in more active ways with school staff, this has often not been the case.

Unfortunately, changing the name from involving to engaging families and communities in schools has not always been associated with shifts in knowledge and power relationships between educators and students' parents and caregivers (Baquedano-Lopez, Alexander, & Hernandez, 2013). Given this tendency, it is more important to pay attention to the nature and quality of the relationships between educators and families rather than only their labels.

When it is genuine, an engagement approach attempts to "flip the script" from an involvement paradigm. Instead of teachers and school staff as the knowledgeable participants, this approach stresses the knowledge that families, community-based organization staff, and community mentors can impart to teachers. The goal of this approach is to create opportunities where teachers can develop an understanding of students', families', and communities' perspectives, "funds of knowledge" (González, Moll, & Amanti, 2005) and community cultural wealth (Yoso, 2005) to help them better see and serve their students.

Weiss, Lopez, and Caspe (2018), in outlining what they claim recent research supports about what is needed in the next generation of family and community engagement with schools, call for a major shift in thinking and a disruption of the power relations that have persisted to date.

> A shift from devaluing and doing to or for families to one of cocreating with them ... involves asking questions, listening, empowering, sharing perspectives and information, partnering, codesigning, implementing, assessing new approaches and solutions, and supporting parent leadership and advocacy for equity and change. (p. 5)

In doing so, they refer to "A Dual Capacity-Building Framework for Family-School Partnerships" that was originally developed by Mapp and Kuttner (2013) and then revised in 2018 (Mapp & Bergman, 2019). This framework outlines both the processes and organizational supports that need to be achieved in order for the collaboration to be genuine, and mutually beneficial in ways that contribute to greater educational justice and community well-being. The processes include interactive, asset-based, culturally responsive, respectful, and collaborative interactions that seek to develop mutual trust among community and school participants over time and that honor family and community expertise and cultural wealth. The organizational supports needed to support this approach include organization leaders who embrace the empowerment of family and community members to play a central role in school decision-making and who put resources into place to support these norm-breaking patterns of family-school partnerships over time. In order for there to be a chance of these goals being achieved, both teacher education and the preparation of education leaders must make family and community partnerships a higher priority in their preparation programs. One challenge for teacher preparation programs is to prepare teachers who are willing and able to engage in these collaborative and mutually beneficial relationships with families and community members.

However, even when there are genuine shifts and a leveling of power between family and community members and educators and where educators are willing to work in collaborative ways, it cannot be taken for granted that teachers will be able to transform what they learn into culturally responsive and sustaining curriculum and pedagogical practices (Sharkey, Olarte, & Ramierez, 2016; Villegas & Lucas, 2002). Or as Smolcic and Katujnich (2017) have put it, intercultural competence and greater knowledge about cultures are not the same things as culturally responsive pedagogy. Teachers need to learn and practice how to integrate community funds of knowledge and cultural wealth into their curriculum and instruction and be mentored in doing so (Hong, 2019).[9]

Preparing Teachers to Teach in Culturally Responsive and Sustaining Ways

Community teachers draw on richly contextualized knowledge of culture, community, and identity in their professional work with children and families in diverse urban communities. . . . Community teachers have a clear sense of their own cultural, political, and racial identities in relation to the children and families they hope to serve. This sense allows them to play a central role in the successful development and education of their students. (Murrell (2000, 2001), p. 4)

There have been many efforts over the years to conceptualize forms of teaching that are culturally based and focused on providing students with an education in which they see themselves and their communities reflected in all aspects of their school experience. These include "culturally congruent teaching" (Au & Kawakami, 1994), "culturally relevant pedagogy" (Ladson-Billings, 2021), "culturally responsive teaching" (Gay, 2018; Villegas & Lucas, 2002), "culturally sustaining pedagogy" (Paris & Alim, 2017), "abolitionist teaching" (Love, 2020), equity pedagogy (Banks & Banks, 1995), "community teaching" (Murrell (2001), and community-based pedagogy (Sharkley, Olarte, & Ramirez, 2016).

These various conceptualizations of a community-focused and culturally based form of teaching that seek to have all students feel affirmed and valued in school emphasize somewhat different aspects of the education process (e.g., curriculum, teaching practices, social relations, the social and political contexts of teaching), and emphasize somewhat different ideas about how teachers should utilize the knowledge they gain about their students and their families and communities. Despite these differences, they all share a common commitment to educating students in nondominant communities in ways that build in positive ways upon the cultural resources that students bring to school with them (e.g., languages, literacies, histories, cultural ways of being) and the funds of knowledge and social practices, and traditions present in their communities. Rather than viewing parents and caregivers as deficient and in need of change by schools, teachers are positioned as learners who can learn to utilize resources in their students' families and communities to help disrupt the patterns of inequitable educational opportunities that have existed in these communities. I will use one of the most recent of these variations of culturally based teaching, "culturally sustaining pedagogy" (CSP) in this book as a signifier for these culturally based approaches to teaching in this book.

> CSP seeks to perpetuate and foster-to sustain-linguistic, literate, and cultural pluralism as part of schooling for social transformation. CSP positions dynamic cultural dexterity as a necessary good, and sees the outcome of learning as additive rather than subtractive, as remaining whole rather than framed as broken, as culturally enriching strengths rather than replacing deficits. Culturally sustaining pedagogy exists wherever education sustains the lifeways of communities who have been and continue to be damaged and erased through schooling. (Paris & Alim, 2017, p. 1)

Munoz (2020) examined research on several conceptualizations of culturally based forms of teaching and developed a framework of eight competencies that she asserts illustrate the various conceptualizations of culturally based teaching that the various versions have in common across grade levels and subject areas. One of the core competencies of culturally based educators that is included in this framework is collaborating with families and the local community. This competency includes a number of dimensions that support the kind of family and community engagement in schools that are either explicitly called for or implied in all of the different versions of culturally based teaching. For example, one aspect of collaborating with families and the local community is that teachers:

> Continually seek to learn more about the local community and families' cultures, values and expectations for their children's education. Further, they see themselves as members of the community and they collaborate with local agencies and organizations to arrange resources that families need. (p. 12)

Because we know from research that CSP is critically important to school success for many students who live in nondominant communities, the question becomes one of learning what can and should be done in teacher preparation programs (e.g., in terms of who they prepare to teach and how they do so) to equip teachers to be able and willing to work in ways that build upon and help sustain the languages, literacies, histories, and cultural practices in the families and communities in which students live. Additionally, we also need to learn what will be needed to build the capacity within teacher preparation programs to do the work that must be done.

The next chapter discusses the evolution of community and teacher education program collaborations in the United States by discussing three significant national projects that took place in the United States over the last seventy plus years that illuminate some of the major sources of variation in the ways in which teacher educators and community members and organizations have worked together to prepare teachers to teach in nondominant communities. Teacher education partnerships with communities also have a long history in other parts of the world that hopefully will be documented by others (e.g., Peterson & Gravett, 2020). The discussion of the details of these traditions is beyond the scope of this book.

Chapter 3 builds on Chapter 2 and elaborates on some of the ways that communities in teacher education (i.e., engaging families and communities in teacher preparation programs and providing community field experiences for prospective teachers), can potentially contribute to the development of community teachers who are willing and able to teach in culturally responsive and sustaining ways. A typology is presented here that identifies the major ways in which teacher candidates have been educated in the broader communities in which their school placement sites exist and the different ways in which parents, caregivers, and community members have been engaged in teacher preparation programs. Examples of these different practices in several counties are briefly discussed.

Then, Chapter 4 discusses what research in several countries has suggested are the design principles that will make it more likely that these efforts will be successful in preparing culturally responsive and sustaining teachers. Although there is merit in identifying the particular dimensions that have reflected the different meanings of communities in teacher preparation programs, the presence of particular activities and people connected to communities in teacher education are not determinative by themselves of the nature and quality of these activities as they are enacted. Activities like spending time in a community-based organization helping students with their homework and mapping community resources can lead to many different outcomes. It is the ways in which these activities are carried out and mediated and what is done with what is learned that matters in determining their nature and quality. The design principles that are articulated in Chapter 4 attempt to offer ways for programs to focus on the things that matter rather than only on the types of activities and interactions.

Also, it is important to note that educational reform, no matter how well carried out, will not bring about educational justice and community well-being alone. It is clear that out-of-school factors play the largest role in influencing educational equity (e.g., Carter & Welner, 2013). I will argue in Chapter 4 that linking educational reform to broader efforts for reform beyond education initiated by organized groups within nondominant communities is the preferable course of action for achieving both educational justice and community well-being.

CHAPTER TWO

An Overview of the Trajectory of Communities in US Teacher Education

As a concept, community is exclusive, vague, rarely defined, complex, contested, and fraught with ambiguity and assumption. (Philip, Way, Garcia, Schuler-Brown & Navarro, 2013, p. 175)
The idea of community constitutes an elastic political construct that holds a variety of contradictory meanings and around which diverse practices occur. (Hill Collins, 2010, p. 7)

The Evolution of Communities in Teacher Education Over Time in the United States

Tracing the broad features of the evolution of communities in US teacher education can provide a basis for articulating some of the major dimensions of variation in how communities have contributed to the preparation of teachers over time and help us begin to understand the different roles that communities have played in teacher education in the

United States and internationally. Work with communities
in colleges and universities, and to a lesser extent in teacher
education programs, in the form of service learning, also has
a long history in other parts of the world both in the Global
North and Global South. Some of this history regarding
the connections between communities and colleges and
universities has been documented in the literature such as
the folk schools in Denmark, Sweden, and Norway (Bagley
& Rust, 2009), the community-based research, Freirean, and
popular education traditions in Latin America universities
(Appe, Rubaii, & Lippez-De Castro, 2017), as well as the
long traditions of university engagement with communities
in Asia and Africa (Peterson & Gravett, 2020). Very little
of the work in these traditions, if they have been applied in
teacher education programs, has been available in mainstream
academic journals and in books published in English. Most
of what I was able to locate in the literature in English on
communities and teacher education programs from countries
other than dominant English-speaking countries like Australia,
Canada, Aotearoa New Zealand, the United Kingdom, and the
United States as well as some non-English-speaking European
countries published in English consist of surveys of the extent
to which teacher education programs prepare teachers for
engaging with families and communities, in a broad way how
they do this preparation (e.g., a course on engaging families
and communities), and how well prepared graduates of teacher
education programs feel in this area (e.g., De Brunie et al.,
2014). With regard to the preparation of teachers to engage
with families and communities in nondominant communities
outside the United States, the work on Indigenous teacher
education programs in Australia, Canada, and Aotearoa
New Zealand is the main body of literature that I was able to
locate that consists of details of the preparation, and in some
cases, discussion of the impact of the preparation on teacher
candidates and Indigenous communities (e.g., Haig-Brown &
Kawehau Hoskins, 2019).[1]

As mentioned in the first chapter, the term "community" in relation to schools refers in this book to the neighborhoods in which students in particular schools live. In the context of teacher education programs, community refers to the neighborhoods served by the schools in which clinical placements are made and to the broader local context (town, city, county) in which these schools are located.

For at least the last seventy years, teacher education scholars in the United States have advocated for the inclusion of community field experiences in the initial preparation of teachers. In 1948, around the time that teacher education programs in the United States began using public schools as sites for clinical teacher education, the American Association of Teachers Colleges issued a report on clinical experiences in teacher education (Flowers, Patterson, Strateymer, & Lindsey, 1948). It is significant that this visible national report at an important time in the history of American teacher education includes community experiences as a necessary and important component of clinical experience.

Modern educators are hopeful of abandoning the concept of the school as an isolated agency in society. They would like to see the school become a community-centered activity. This places new responsibilities on the shoulders of teachers and/or on those responsible for their preservice education. It means professional laboratory experiences directed toward helping the intended teacher understand what is involved in building effective community relationships both as a teacher and as a citizen of the community. For a prospective teacher, these may include experiences in working with parents, using community agencies and resources as they contribute to the ongoing activities of the group, studying the community to better understand learners' needs and backgrounds, working cooperatively with other educational agencies in the interests of children, and contributing with children or youth to community activities. (Flowers, Patterson, Strateymer, & Lindsey, 1948, p. 27)

At the beginning of this new era for clinical experiences in teacher education in the United States when clinical experiences began to move from university campus laboratory schools to public schools, the call for the inclusion of community experiences was based on a general argument about the importance of student teachers learning about their students' communities as a resource for curriculum and classroom instruction (Hogdon & Saunders, 1951). For example, in a 1964 report published by the Association for Student Teaching Blair and Erickson (1964) argue:

> Too often a student teacher completes student teaching without realizing his [sic] personal and professional opportunities and obligations in the community. Professional literature in the field of education and school administration should increase emphasis on the importance of knowing and utilizing the community and its resources in designing the school curriculum and in planning learning experiences. It is imperative that more conscious efforts be made to study and utilize the resources of the community during the student teaching experience. (p. viii)

Over time, as the composition of public school students in the United States became more diverse racially, linguistically, and culturally, the percentage of students in public schools living in poverty and racial and class segregation in schools continued to increase. As a multicultural teacher education movement began to grow across the United States teacher education community from the mid-1970s on (Baptiste, Baptiste, & Gollnick, 1980), calls for community experience in teacher education began to shift in their focus. Instead of the generic endorsement of learning how to work with students' parents/ caregivers and learning about their students' communities beginning in the late 1960s, rhetoric about community experience in teacher education began to be focused on learning to teach in historically marginalized and oppressed communities in more culturally and community responsive ways that support greater equity in learning opportunities and outcomes (Ladson-Billings, 1995). Since then, it has been argued by some that a community-engaged approach to teacher education prepares teachers "with the capacity to connect the content they are responsible for teaching to children's lived experience rendering learning more authentic, relevant, and engaging" (Zygmunt, Cipollone, Clark, & Tancock, 2018, p. 6).

Although the multicultural movement in teacher education was beginning to result in the inclusion of courses on language and culture in teacher education programs, some advocates of a multicultural orientation to preparing teachers clearly asserted that although coursework was needed to prepare teachers who could successfully educate the increasingly diverse student population in US schools, coursework by itself was inadequate and that community experiences were needed. In other words, these courses were necessary but not sufficient. Hayes (1980) explains:

> To interject a few language and culture courses into a preservice or inservice training program is not enough. Clinical experiences should be designed with opportunities for students to observe and participate in community oriented learning. Field-based activities could include work in day-care centers, recreation centers, youth employment training, and alternative education programs. (p. 107)

In addition to calls for community experiences for teacher preparation programs, the dialogue was also broadened to include calls for community engagement in the governance and implementation of teacher education programs. This meant that the value of community engagement and community experience began to be justified in ways that included the need to better prepare middle class and in the United States the mostly White and monolingual English-speaking teachers who continued to make up the majority of the US teaching force to be more successful with students living in communities highly impacted by structural racism and poverty. These communities were very much unlike those that many teacher candidates had experienced in their lives (Smith, 1969).

Also, during this period, nondominant communities in urban areas increased their organized efforts to gain a genuine voice in how the schools in their communities were run, by whom, and how their children were being taught (e.g., Featherstone, 1968). These organized efforts within nondominant communities to increase community influence on how their children were taught also began to be focused on greater community influence on how teachers were prepared to teach in schools within their communities.

Three Important Examples

Three examples described here from the United States illustrate this shift from an approach to preparing teachers to work with families and communities in general to a social-justice-oriented approach focused on working with nondominant communities with the aim of helping to ameliorate the growing inequities in learning opportunities and outcomes for children going to school in different communities: (1) the emergence of the Teacher Corps; (2) the report published in 1969 by the Teacher Education Task Force of the National Institute for Advanced Study in Teaching Disadvantaged Youth; and (3) the report published in 1976 by the National Study Commission on Undergraduate Education and the Preparation of Teachers.

The Teacher Corps (1965–81)

In 1965, the US federal government authorized the Teacher Corps (TC) as part of its first-ever federal Higher Education Act. The goals of the TC were twofold: to strengthen the educational experiences in public schools for children living in urban and rural communities with a concentration of poverty and to help broaden teacher education programs to improve their ability to prepare teachers to teach successfully and stay over time in these communities (Graham, 1970). Building on the Cardozo Project in Urban Teaching, an innovative teacher education program in the Washington DC public schools that was originally designed to prepare returned Peace Corps[2] volunteers as teachers (Graham, 1968; Rogers, 2009), TC adopted a tripartite model of preparation that focused on contributions from the university, schools, and local communities in the preparation of teachers. There were approximately 75–100 individual Teacher Corps projects at any given time in urban and rural communities throughout the country. Significantly, the Teacher Corps required community participation in the governance and planning of the individual projects, and about one-quarter of the time of interns was spent working in the communities served by their internship school collaborating on projects with community members that were decided on by the community. In many of the sites, interns were strongly encouraged or required to live in one of the neighborhoods served by their internship school during their preparation.

Each of the local Teacher Corps projects was governed by a steering committee and school community council that included equal representation of schools, universities, and communities. The message of the Teacher Corps for the field of teacher preparation in the United States included, but also went far beyond, the importance of providing community experiences to enable interns to know about the communities in which their students live and to become able and willing to integrate this knowledge and community expertise into their work in the classroom. It also went beyond the idea of helping interns learn how to work in respectful ways with their students' families. The Teacher Corps example suggested that families and communities that are supposed to be served by public schools have a right to have a genuine voice and participate in decision-making in their children's schools and in the teacher education programs that prepare teachers for their communities.[3] The definition of community member in the Teacher Corps did not focus on community elites, such as prominent community leaders, but rather on "grassroots community representatives" such as parents/caregivers and members of community organizations and advocacy groups within nondominant communities (Masla & Royster, 1976).

During the life of the Teacher Corps, a national survey of teacher education programs indicated that there were very few teacher education programs in the United States that included local communities in program governance, planning, and instruction except in the Teacher Corps, and in a few other federally funded programs when it was mandated by funders.

> It quickly became apparent through a survey that higher education programs for preparing teachers which require community involvement and/or community training were barely existent except in cases of federally funded programs. (Masla & Royster, 1976, p. 83)

The intent of the community component in Teacher Corps was to push teacher education programs in higher education institutions to do three things: (1) broaden the idea of clinical experiences to include carefully mentored community experiences as an important site for teacher learning; (2) engage grassroots community members in the governance, decision-making, and instruction in teacher education programs; (3) contribute to the possibility of greater genuine collaboration between educators and family and community members in nondominant communities in the preparation of teachers who would be knowledgeable of the expertise and cultural wealth in their students' communities and use this knowledge and the support of community members to provide a more culturally responsive form of education to their children. The central philosophy of the TC could be encapsulated in the following way:

> Educators and citizens must form an inseparable
> partnership; this holds for teacher educators as well; in
> order to develop preparation programs that will produce a
> *community oriented teacher*. These partners must be clear
> about their roles as mutually supportive partners. (Masla &
> Royster, 1976, p. 1)

Although a variety of financial and political problems that
were associated with the Teacher Corps over its sixteen-year
existence prevented the program from transforming university
teacher education or school-community relationships in
nondominant communities as its founders had hoped (e.g.,
Edelfelt, Corwin, & Hanna, 1974), the ambitious goals of the
program during these sixteen years had a clear impact on two
subsequent national commissions that sought to reimagine
teacher education in the United States to educate teachers for
nondominant communities.

The Report of the National Institute
for Advanced Study in Teaching
Disadvantaged Youth (1976)

About the same time as the Teacher Corps was initiated, the
NDEA was established in 1966 by the US Office of Education.
The contract was awarded to the American Association of
Colleges for Teacher Education who then subcontracted the
work of the institute to Ball State University in Indiana which
organized a national task force composed of educators from
university Education Schools and school districts. The goal of
this task force was similar to the charge of the Teacher Corps: to
develop new ideas and a plan for US teacher education programs
to educate teachers more successfully to teach students living in
communities highly impacted by poverty. The final report of
this group, "Teachers for the Real World" (Smith, 1969), was
published after the task force's three years of work.

This task force, like the Teacher Corps, emphasized the important role for local communities, in partnership with universities and schools, in the planning and operation of teacher education programs. Significantly, it did not uncritically idealize and oversimplify the task of fostering community collaboration in teacher preparation as had been and continues to be common. On the contrary, the task force recognized the inevitable complications associated with defining the community, who speaks for it, and what things it wants, as well as the complexity involved in university faculty, school educators, and community members collaborating together because of the different worlds in which they live. In the end, it placed much of the responsibility on university teacher educators for practicing what they preached. As Smith (1969) explained: "Faculty people have to learn therefore, how to involve community members early in the planning stage rather than later, and how to demonstrate their own sincerity rather than merely talk about it" (p. 97).

As was the case with the Teacher Corps, the emphasis on community participation in teacher education in the task force report did not result in widespread impact on teacher education programs. Smith (1980), who was one of the task force members, revisited the themes in the task force report a decade later in a widely discussed monograph that he wrote with funding from the US Department of Education elaborating on the themes articulated in the 1969 report. Both here and in the original task force report, the link to the work of the Teacher Corps was made clear.

> From the beginning, the training facility has been thought of as a particular school in which the trainees gain experience. This conception must be abandoned. The Teacher Corps has taught in no uncertain language that the community and its schools constitute the training laboratory. The pioneer work of the Teacher Corps in creating a new setting for the training of teachers has now begun to be realized as one of the most significant developments in recent decades. (Smith, 1980, pp. 23–24)

Report of the Study Commission on Undergraduate Education and Teacher Education

Teacher Education in the United States: The Responsibility Gap

A third visible example of a national effort to transform US teacher education to become more community inclusive and responsive came in 1976 in a report and in several papers commissioned by a study commission (e.g., Olson et al., 1975) funded by the US Department of Health, Education and Welfare. According to the assistant secretary of the department who introduced the report to the nation in a brief letter, the intent of the study commission's report was to address "the extent to which communities should be responsible for the content of pre-service and in-service preparation of teachers" (p. vii). The concern here, as was the case with the Teacher Corps and the NDEA task force, was particularly with communities that had been highly impacted by poverty. The committee consisted of arts and science and education faculty from universities across the country and a few representatives from school districts and community-based organizations active in education.

One of the major recommendations of the study commission was to call for a strong role for communities in program governance, planning, and instruction in the education of teachers. For example, it called for the development of formal governance processes which give parents and communities a major role in the education and certification of teachers and determining the role of schools in the community and the community in the schools (Study Commission, 1976, p. 156).

One of the main reasons why the study commission argued that teacher education programs should engage members of their local communities in their programs was to disrupt the cycle of young missionary-oriented teachers coming into nondominant communities to try and save students from their allegedly broken communities. It was hoped that the engagement of local community members in all aspects of teacher education programs would help screen missionary-motivated teachers out of the teaching profession.

In the "school-university-based teacher education" programs (Olson et al., 1975) that the study commission hoped would result from the infusion of federal funding into the development of a strong role for communities in the preparation of teachers, the community's role would not be limited to participation in governance and planning, but would also result in community members providing direct "cultural input" into programs that would enable new teachers to acquire the dispositions and skills needed to understand the communities in which they are teaching from the perspectives of community members.

> School-based professional training should include a strong component of teaching by the community and control by parents and students. It should respect the lifestyle, value system, language, and expressive system of the culture in which the school that provides the teaching is located. Both teacher teams and IHE faculty should respond to these cultural aspects. (Study Commission, 1976, p. 11)

Another important issue that was raised by the study commission was to distinguish between genuine community participation in teacher education programs and that which was mere tokenism. There has been some evidence over the years that when community members have participated in various aspects of teacher education programs, the collaboration has been superficial, not altering existing power relationships that privilege universities and schools, and where community participants often do not feel that their ideas and suggestions are valued and listened to by all of their university and school counterparts.

For example, Popkewitz (1979) examined community engagement in one Teacher Corps site in Wisconsin and documented the ways in which university teacher educators and school representatives subtly marginalized community participants, in part, through the use of professional language. He argued that community participation in teacher education can sometimes serve as a subtle way to support stability rather than change in power structures and fail to give community members greater voice in schools and teacher education programs. It has been argued that this kind of superficial collaboration with communities in teacher preparation has been very common (Also see Barnes, 2017; Guillen & Zeichner, 2018; Lees, 2016; Clark, Zygmunt, & Cipollone, 2021) This situation is similar to the ways in which family involvement and engagement in schools in nondominant communities has often maintained the privileging of professional education expertise and the continued marginalization of family and community expertise under the guise of community empowerment (Baquedano, Alexander, & Hernandez, 2013; Ishimaru, 2019). It is not only important who is in the room and seated at the table. Also important is the quality of how people interact with each other and whose knowledge counts in these interactions.

Cook & Kothari (2001) have referred to the manipulation that sometimes results from this type of more subtle control and stability under the guise of democratic participation as "the new tyranny." Whether it is consciously or unconsciously done, what distinguishes "the new tyranny" from more authentic forms of participation is whether an epistemological shift has occurred in whose knowledge counts in the participatory process (Harfatt, 2019). Hyland and Meacham (2004) have argued that university teacher educators:

> Must learn how to reexamine their programs and yield some of their intellectual territory to create a community-knowledge-centered model that privileges the historically subjugated knowledge of community groups. (p. 130)

1980s–Today

Following these three examples, efforts to push teacher education programs and policymakers in the United States to provide a strong role for nondominant communities in the preparation of teachers for their communities have not often been reflected in subsequent national teacher education reform projects or in influential national reports that examined the status of teacher education and made recommendations for the future. They also have not been reflected in the practices in most teacher education programs in the United States and internationally. For example, none of the major national reform projects in the United States such as the Holmes Group Partnership (2007), the National Network for Educational Renewal (Goodlad, 1998), or the Council for Chief State School Officers Network for Transforming Educator Preparation (CSSO, 2012), all of which sought to transform teacher education nationally, made the issue of community engagement in preparing teachers a major aspect of their reform agendas. Although at least some, if not most, of the major reform efforts in the last few decades have emphasized the need to strengthen school-university partnerships in teacher preparation, they have oftentimes ignored the role of communities in teacher education partnerships while ironically at the same time acknowledging the importance of the school-family-community connection to student learning (Murrell, 2001, 1998). The one possible exception to this conclusion is the over $100 million-dollar national reform effort funded by the Carnegie Corporation and others, "Teachers for a New Era." Although the core emphases of this project that were implemented in eleven different sites across the country did not include community participation in the project framework that delineated the things that all of the sites promised to address with their funding, a comprehensive analysis of the impact of this work (McDiarmid & Caprino, 2017) included the following conclusion among the small set of recommendations from the project:

Efforts to improve teacher preparation must reach beyond the institution-not just K-12 schools, but communities as well. Some sites felt that their community partners were as critical to the work as their school partners. In some cases, community organizations played a role in preparing candidates to work in culturally diverse communities. Understanding the communities where they teach is vital to teacher success. Community voices need to be heard from the start and community leaders need to be engaged throughout. (p. 174)

The two most recent national reports on clinical experiences in teacher education in the United States (AACTE, 2018; NCATE, 2010) define clinical experiences as existing in schools, and only briefly mention, but do not develop, the idea of communities being part of the school-university partnerships. Although it has been relatively easy to find broad statements by individuals or small groups of teacher educators about the value of engaging communities in teacher education programs like the following example from one of the former editors of the *Journal of Teacher Education*, the engagement of local communities in programs is relatively uncommon in the United States and internationally.

The more we can involve community partners who on a daily basis are more involved with the ongoing issues of the community and the lives of its members, the more likely we are to be able to prepare those who are committed to and prepared for the contexts in which they will be teaching. (Richmond, 2017, p. 7)

Many Brief Attempts, but Very Few Long Long-Lasting Examples

The community partnership work that has existed in teacher education in the United States has been conducted and written about by relatively few individuals and has usually only been sustained for a short time either without additional resources or with temporary grant funds. The longevity of this work has often been dependent on the continuing presence of the particular individuals in programs and communities who initiated the partnerships. These efforts have usually been small and short-lived and have involved college/university partnerships with various community organizations and groups such as community-based service organizations (e.g., Lees, 2016; McDonald, Bowman, & Brayko, 2013), religious organizations (e.g., Seidel & Friend, 2002), community activists and organizations (e.g., Zeichner, Bowman, Napolitan, & Guillen, 2016), neighborhood associations (e.g., Skinner, Garreton, & Schultz, 2011) and Indigenous tribes (e.g., Archibald, 2015).

There have been only a handful of programs in the United States where genuine and reciprocal community engagement has persisted over a long period of time. One example of such a program is the Associated Colleges of the Midwest *Urban Education Program* (Sconzert, Lazzetto, & Purkey, 2000; Zeichner & Melnick, 1996b). This program included community immersion for a semester or a year-long student teaching placement (depending on the number of certifications sought by teacher candidates) and substantial informal and formal instruction by community members. It prepared students from midwestern liberal arts colleges to teach in Chicago Public Schools beginning in 1963 and lasted for forty-seven years.

Another enduring example of communities in teacher education, the *Navajo Nation Project*, involves a partnership between Indiana University's School of Education and the Navajo nation. This program, like the Urban Education Program, involves a semester to a year of community immersion that includes student teaching and substantial learning from Navajo community members. The first placements in this program (formerly called the American Indian Reservation Project) were made in 1972, and it has continued to place teacher candidates from Indiana University and others across the country for over fifty years (Mahan, 1993; Stachowski & Mahan, 1998; Zeichner & Melnick, 1996a).

Also, in British Columbia, Canada, NITEP, *The Indigenous Teacher Education Program* involves a partnership between the Faculty of Education at the University of British Columbia and the First Nations Education Council that developed and monitors the program. This program began in 1974 and is still preparing Indigenous teachers for First Nations Communities in BC. (Archibald, 2015). Another Indigenous program in the United States, the *Indigenous Roots Teacher Education Program,* is a 24-year-old partnership in Nebraska involving the Little Priest Tribal College, the University of Nebraska, and six Indigenous communities.

Currently, there are a small number of teacher education programs in the United States that have been working to include community expertise and cultural wealth in their preparation of teachers for a decade or more. These include programs such as Illinois State University's *Chicago Teacher Education Pipeline*, which began in 2004 that at one point involved partnerships between the School of Education at Illinois State University, the Chicago Public Schools, and community-based organizations in five neighborhoods in Chicago. This program is now offered through Illinois State's National Center for Urban Education and has recently expanded to also include partnerships in two nearby cities Decatur and Peoria. It involves an optional four-week homestay and school and community experience during the summer before student teaching for a semester that includes mentoring by community members. One interesting aspect of this program is that it has funded many of the faculty who teach the courses in the program to spend time in the neighborhoods in Chicago, Decatur, and Peoria where teacher candidates complete their student teaching learning about these communities from community members. The faculty then revise their courses to be more relevant to these communities (Lee, 2018; Mustian, O'Mally, Garcia, Millan, & Zamudio-Mainou, 2021).

Another highly visible example in the United States is the Ball State University's *Schools Within the Context of Community* program that began in the fall of 2009 that includes an optional semester of coursework and clinical experience in two schools in a particular community that partners with the program for more than a decade. A subset of elementary teacher candidates have experienced this program option each year. Community members and families mentor teacher candidates, and in one case, a community member teaches a course in the program (Clark, Zygmunt, Tancock, & Cipollone, 2021; Zygmunt & Clark, 2015).

In 2015, faculty and community partners at Ball State organized a small network of teacher education programs that have made efforts to engage local community members in their teacher education programs to learn from each other's work, *The Alliance for Community Engaged Teacher Preparation* which includes at least one program from outside the United States (Clark, Zygmunt, Tancock, & Cipollone, 2021). Ball State faculty also organized a special interest group for individuals in the American Association for Colleges of Teacher Education (AACTE), *Community-Engaged Teacher Preparation*. More recently, in 2019, the non-profit organization "National Association for Family, School, and Community Engagement" (NAFSCE) organized and launched the "Pre-service Family Engagement Consortium" involving programs and school and community partners in seven states.[4] In 2022, this same organization offered small grants to up to seven collaboratives of programs and partners to engage in short-term efforts to prepare teachers for family and community engagement in diverse communities.[5] All three of these efforts by AACTE and NAFSCE were aimed at stimulating more work in teacher preparation programs in preparing teachers to engage families and communities and in disseminating the work of these programs to others.

Preparing Teachers to Work with Families and Communities

Despite these examples, many if not most teacher candidates receive little or no preparation for working with families and communities as part of their preparation for teaching. Both in the United States and internationally, preparing teachers to work with families and communities in urban and rural areas that have been historically marginalized has been the exception rather than the rule in initial teacher education programs (e.g., Cooper, 2007; de Bruine et al., 2014; Dobber et al., 2013; Epstein & Sanders, 2006; Gomila, Pascual, & Quincoces, 2018; Mutton, Burn, & Thompson, 2018).

The lack of attention to this issue in many teacher education programs is confirmed by the results of surveys in the United States and Europe where graduates of TPPs are asked how well they believe they were prepared in particular aspects of teaching. Preparation to work with students' families and to know about their communities is often cited as one of the areas where teacher candidates feel they have had the least preparation (Graue, 2005). This lack of attention to preparing teachers to work with families and communities is also true in other parts of the world such as in Africa and Australia. In Europe, Thompson, Willemse, Mutton, Burn, & deBruine, 2018 conclude:

> Given the importance of family school partnerships, it might be assumed that programs of initial teacher education would emphasize it within their programs, but research has shown that process is often haphazard and inadequate. It is therefore not surprising that beginning teachers regard collaborating with parents as one of the major challenges they face and one for which they do not feel adequately prepared. (p. 259)

In Australia, a 2014 study by Saltmarsh, Barr, & Chapman (2015) of how issues related to parent-school engagement were being addressed in teacher preparation across the country appeared to challenge the conclusion that international preparation programs pay little or no attention to this important issue. This Australian study found that "there was considerable variation between teacher education programs in both the extent to which the topic of parent-school engagement is addressed" (p.

16), and in the ways in which it was addressed. Overall, the authors of this study concluded that despite a clear commitment in programs to developing teacher candidates' understanding of the importance of family and community relationships, "there was insufficient continuity to ensure that all beginning teachers have a thorough understanding of how to work with families and communities" (p. 1). The authors cited the difficulties in making room in a crowded curriculum for this work as one of the factors responsible for the insufficiency of preparation in this area. They also note that many teachers in Australia typically identify working with families and communities as the area where they most feel they need more preparation.

In another study of teacher education institutions in Finland, Alanko (2018) suggests that the attention to preparing teachers to work with families and communities provides a more positive picture than in other countries because, in part, the teacher educators surveyed considered their graduates to be rather competent to work with pupil's families, but she then goes on to caution readers about making any generalizations from the limited data collected. Although the survey indicated that the majority of programs in Finland appeared to include material about family and community partnerships in their curricula, Alanko (2018) encourages programs to work actively with schools providing clinical training to teacher candidates in order to guarantee opportunities for novices to interact with pupils' families, implying that this may be a problem.

Orland-Barak and Laurenteva's (2019) examination of global trends in teacher education programs between 2000 and 2018 confirms these conclusions from Australia, the United States, and Europe about the lack of adequate attention to preparing teachers to work with families and communities. Although they identify the creation of school-community-university partnerships as one of the six major trends in teacher education during this time period, they conclude that despite the importance of these partnerships in program and government agency visions for teacher education programs globally, "there is no evident satisfactory picture of family-school partnership provisions within initial teachers education or in the preparedness of student teachers to deal with a variety of complex social and cultural issues" (p. 7). Additionally, most of the assessments of to what extent and how teacher education programs in the United States and internationally do not differentiate between different kinds of communities in reporting their data. Even though there may be attention to working with families and communities in a teacher education program in a general way, this does not guarantee that nondominant communities are included in this work. Also, just because there may be attention to working with families and communities in preparing teachers, this preparation does not necessarily include experiences in communities for candidates or opportunities for family and community members to contribute directly to the preparation process or participate in monitoring the quality of the preparation.

A recent survey by the National Association for Family, School and Community Engagement in the United States found that initial state teacher certification requirements in only 30 percent of the fifty-six states and territories include the foundational elements identified as essential for successful family engagement. Less than 40 percent of state certification requirements address the need for teachers to establish strong relationships and trust with families (National Association for Family, School, and Community Engagement, 2020). A more recent survey by NAFCE indicates that the lack of attention to family and community engagement in state teacher certification requirements has undermined the attention to this issue in teacher education programs in the United States.[6] Additionally, because state teaching standards do not often include more than superficial attention to working with families and communities, state program approval systems and national teacher preparation program accreditation processes, until recently, have given little or no attention to community engagement in teacher preparation programs.

There are two national program accreditation agencies for teacher education programs in the United States: the Council for the Accreditation of Educator Programs (CAEP) and the Association for Advancing Quality in Educator Preparation (AAQEP). Beginning in 2022, the larger of these organizations, CAEP, revised its program approval standards to include explicit mention of working with families and community engagement in its standards across several categories of its accreditation rubric (e.g., content and pedagogical knowledge, clinical partnerships, and practice). Similarly, AAQEP has included attention in one of its program accreditation standards teachers candidates' abilities to work with families and communities in a variety of cultural and socioeconomic community contexts (Caspe, Malina, & Finklea, 2021).

Although Caspe, Monaco, and Finklea (2021) acknowledge that currently there is great variation within and among programs in the United States in whether family and community engagement is treated as a fundamental priority or simply seen as an "add on," they argue that these recent efforts by the two national teacher education accreditation agencies in the United States "create the infrastructure for a more systemic and robust approach to the preparation of educators for family engagement" (p. 2).

One issue that is not addressed in these optimistic projections is the ways in which teacher educators define and enact community engagement in the preparation of teachers in different contexts. Although the degree to which family and community engagement are prioritized in programs is important, what teacher educators mean by family and community engagement and what they do are just as, if not, more important. Over time, family and community engagement has meant a lot of different things in teacher education programs. In the next chapter, a typology is presented to illustrate some of the most important dimensions of variation in how these terms have been defined and used in teacher education.

CHAPTER THREE

Various Interpretations of Communities in Teacher Education

Since the beginning of discussions about the role of communities in teacher education, there has been widespread use of general slogans such as "community experience," "community partnerships," "community participation," "community involvement," and "community engagement" to describe work in the field. Similarly, many different terms such as "community-engaged" teacher education, "community-focused" teacher education, "community-dedicated" teacher education, "community-centered" teacher education, "community knowledge-centered" teacher education, "community-based" teacher education, and "community-oriented" teacher education appear in the literature on community participation and community experiences in teacher preparation programs. Frequently, the most important qualities of this work have not been explicated. One consequence of this situation is there is widespread confusion about the specific meaning of these terms, and the practice has become common of equating work that is motivated by different purposes and represents different qualities of integration of community expertise and cultural wealth into teacher preparation programs. As mentioned previously, there have also been attempts by teacher educators and researchers to declare community-focused work in teacher preparation as a new idea or as an approach when in fact the ideas involved are neither new nor representative of a singular approach.

The following typology (see Figure 3.1) identifies three dimensions that portray the type of work that has gone in within the umbrella of communities in teacher education in the United States and internationally. First, it presents a set of three areas that address the question of what it is that families and communities participate in when they contribute to teacher education and the nature and quality of their participation. Next, it identifies four areas that address the major dimensions of variation in the nature of teacher candidate participation in community field experiences during their teacher preparation programs.

Although these two aspects of the framework address the preparation of all teachers for teaching in nondominant

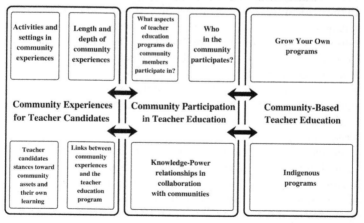

FIGURE 3.1 *Community participation in teacher education.*

communities (those candidates who come from nondominant communities and those who do not), in reality, they mostly focus on preparing outsiders to teach "other people's children" in nondominant communities which are often foreign to the outsiders' own life experiences (Delpit, 1988). In order to capture the full range of work that has gone on in initial teacher education programs with regard to communities, it is also necessary to discuss the third dimension of the framework that addresses the efforts that have existed to specifically recruit and prepare teacher candidates from nondominant communities, including a specific focus, in many cases, on BIPOC teachers, to teach in these communities through the development of special programs designed specifically for these individuals.[1] Two types of community-based teacher education programs are discussed here: "Grow Your Own" programs and Indigenous teacher education programs.

As we have seen from the brief overview of the evolution of communities in teacher education in the United States in Chapter 2, members of local communities have participated in different aspects of teacher education programs and teacher candidates have had very different kinds of experiences in their programs with families and communities, if they have them at all. In order to begin to understand how communities in teacher education can potentially enhance the quality of the preparation of teachers who will teach in nondominant communities and the characteristics of community participation and community experiences for teacher candidates that support the preparation of community-oriented teachers who teach in culturally responsive and sustaining ways, we must understand the dimensions of variation among different instances of community experience and community participation in mainstream teacher education programs, and in the programs to recruit and prepare teachers from nondominant communities. This will enable us to begin to differentiate one instance from another and to help us understand how the particulars of community participation, community experience, and community-based teacher preparation programs matter in teacher learning and practice and ultimately in the quality and equity of student learning. In reality, the term "communities" in teacher education is a contested concept that varies across and within programs depending on how certain issues of knowledge and power are resolved by participants.

The Nature and Quality of Community Participation in TPPs

How Do Family and Community Members Participate in Teacher Education Programs?

The first dimension of variation with regard to community participation in TPPs relates to which aspects of teacher preparation programs community members participate in. As was the case in the Teacher Corps and a few other federally funded teacher education programs in the United States such as the "Trainer of Teacher Trainers" program (Hawley & Vellanti, 1970), community members have sometimes participated in the governance and evaluation of teacher education programs. Serving on an advisory committee has been one major form of community participation in program governance. Some programs though have gone beyond merely including community members on advisory and governing councils and committees and have included them in the ongoing organization, planning, and evaluation of programs, courses, and clinical experiences. Additionally, some programs have also included community members as guest speakers, co-instructors, or instructors in program courses and seminars or as mentors of teacher candidates. Sometimes this instructional work is carried out by community members who are hired as adjuncts to teach specific courses or to participate in particular events such as community panels, and sometimes programs have established staff positions in teacher education programs for community members as in the cases of Ball State University in the United States and La Trobe University in Australia (Clark, Zygmunt, Tancock, & Cipollone, 2021; Lampert, 2021). Sometimes community members are asked to contribute to teacher education programs without financial compensation, and sometimes they are compensated for their contributions. In a few cases, in community-based Grow Your Own (GYO) and Indigenous programs, community members have participated in the development of the criteria used to select individuals into a program and in the process of candidate selection (Rogers-Ard, 2017; Van Winkle, 2017).

Who in the Community Participates in Teacher Education Programs?

Another issue related to community participation in teacher education programs is concerned with the question of who in the community participates in programs and what perspectives within the community they represent. Philip, Way, Garcia, Schuler-Brown, and Navarro (2013) note the tendency among educators to talk about communities in ways that fail to recognize the diversity in members' backgrounds and perspectives that exists in all communities. In order to understand the participation of communities in teacher education in specific programs, we need to know about who the community members and/or organizations are that participate in a program, how they came to this work, and what groups and perspectives they reflect within the broader community. Some teacher education programs like the Chicago Teacher Education Pipeline and the Ball State School within the Context of Community Program in the United States have developed long-term partnerships with particular community organizations within specific neighborhoods (Mustian, O'Mally, Garcia, Millan, & Zamudio-Mainou, 2021; Zygmunt & Clark, 2015). Others, like teacher educators at the University of Washington, developed partnerships with particular community activists and organizations citywide, and with the collaboration of the activists and community organization staff, they engaged community members from many neighborhoods across a large city and surrounding towns in the preparation of teachers (e.g., Guillen & Zeichner, 2018; McDonald, Bowman, & Brako, 2013; Zeichner, Bowman, Guillen, & Napolitan, 2016). Some programs have involved partnerships with particular religious organizations in a community (Seidel & Friend, 2002) or with specific Indigenous tribes or community organizations serving tribal communities or refugee communities (e.g., Lees, 2016; Naido & Brace, 2017).

A variety of different kinds of people have also been involved or engaged with TPPs including community educators, community leaders, activists and elders, parents and grandparents, business owners, farmers and sheepherders, nurses, local artists, and so on. In one unusual example of community mentors of teacher candidates that was initiated by community members to contribute to disrupting the school-to-prison pipeline[2] teacher residents in the Seattle Teacher Residency Program meet several times during their year-long program with members of the Black Prisoners Caucus at the Monroe Correctional facility near Seattle.[3] The members of this caucus help teacher residents see the consequences of the pipeline and to reflect on the stories of the caucus members about their school experiences and how these experiences contributed to them making poor choices that resulted in them being incarcerated. The men provide advice to the novice teachers (and also to teacher educators) about how to support their students in ways that were lacking in their own schooling.

In Australia, teacher educators in a program at La Trobe University have sought to engage Indigenous refugees, poor, and other historically vulnerable communities in central rather than token ways in preparing teachers to teach in their communities. Teacher educators developed a three-stage strategy for developing relationships with community members. This strategy involves starting with approaching easily accessible community organizations and leaders, followed by conversations with individual community members or informal community groups. The third and final stage involves engaging with marginalized individuals who are rarely consulted by educators. The goal here is for the university teacher educators to be able to move through the stages by demonstrating that they can be trusted by community members and that their rhetoric about co-shaping the program with community members is genuine (Lampert, 2021).

Sometimes the invitation to partner in preparing teachers is initiated by teacher educators as in this La Trobe University example. At other times, such as in the case of the Logan Square Neighborhood Association Grow Your Own Program in Chicago, communities initiate the connection and invite university preparation programs to partner with them to prepare teachers for their neighborhood schools (e.g., Skinner, Garreton, & Schultz, 2011). Forming connections with potential family and community partners in preparing teachers is a process that should be carefully thought through on both sides because of the importance of the quality of the relationships that are developed to the quality of teacher education and community partnerships.

Knowledge-Power Relationships in Community Participation

Probably the most important aspect of community participation in teacher education is the quality of the knowledge and power relationships that exist between school, program, and community participants in a program. As was seen in the first chapter that discussed school and community relationships in nondominant communities, we know very little about the nature and quality of these relationships unless we examine questions such as: Whose voices are heard and have influence, and whose agendas are addressed in the work that is done within these partnerships? Who conceptualizes the work and plans it, and when are the partners brought into the process and under what conditions? In short, whose knowledge counts? Who are identified as the teacher educators is important since in some teacher education partnerships community participants are framed as "guests" who are permitted by the "real" teacher educators to contribute to the preparation of teachers.

There has often been a big difference between the quality of teacher education partnerships at the surface level of the rhetoric that is used by teacher educators to describe them and what is revealed through a deeper analysis of the knowledge and power relationships that they contain (Bortolin, 2011). There is much evidence that many of the partnerships that have existed in teacher education have ignored the role of nondominant local communities in preparing teachers (e.g., Delany-Barmann, 2010; Murrell, 1998; Souto-Manning & Martell, 2019; Zeichner, 2021).

Even when nondominant community members and organizations have been included in teacher education partnerships, these partnerships have often been predominantly university or program centric rather than community-centric (Zeichner, Payne, & Brayko, 2015). The role of community members has often been severely limited to providing input within boundaries clearly established by program faculty. There is a big difference between "informing" predetermined goals and participating in the conceptualization and design of those goals (Ishimaru et al., 2019). Furthermore, the use of terms such as "community engagement," which suggests that community members have a greater role in shaping the collaboration agenda than the term "community involvement," has not always accurately reflected the reality of the second-class citizen role for community participants and their communities who are still positioned as recipients of the expertise of the university faculty (Shay & Lambert, 2020).

Building on the work discussed in the first chapter that distinguished community and family *involvement* in schools from *engagement* (e.g., Calabrese-Barton, Drake, Perez, St. Louis, & George, 2004; Hong, 2011), we will now examine an approach to distinguishing the nature and quality of knowledge-power relationships between families and communities and teacher education program faculty and staff.

Involving Communities in Teacher Education Programs

Probably the most common way that community members have participated in teacher education programs has been as representatives on advisory committees where they attend periodic meetings with faculty and listen to faculty presentations about the work being done in programs. In these cases, the agendas of the meetings are most often set by university/program faculty and the community members' roles are limited mostly to listening and sharing their reactions to what is presented. The amount of floor time during these meetings is often monopolized by the university/non-university program faculty, and staff, and community members are often positioned as reactors to what has been framed for them by program teacher educators. Involving communities in teacher education programs has also included guest speaking appearances by community members in program courses where the community member's participation is limited to responding to the specific requests asked for in their invitation. Sometimes, however, when community members are asked to speak with a class of teacher candidates, they are given greater latitude in deciding what they will talk about and how they will do so.

One example of this later situation is from the elementary teacher education program at the University of Washington a few years ago where at the beginning of each cohort's experience in the program, a panel of parents and caregivers from the nondominant communities in which most of the TCs were placed for the year met with the cohorts and talked about their experiences as parents and caregivers and their children's experiences as students with teachers in the local public schools and what their hopes and dreams are for the education of their children (Zeichner, Bowman, Guillen, & Napolitan, 2016). In this example, and others like it (also see Scaife & Zygmunt, 2021), community members have broad latitude to discuss topics that are connected to the coursework in the program in the ways that they want to discuss them, and in some cases, they also help decide the topics and participate in the framing of the sessions. However, involving families and communities in teacher education programs generally provides those from the community with very limited discretion with regard to their input. An extreme example of this situation is when a session is framed by the university teacher educator(s) and community members are given a list of the specific points that they should cover in their presentation to TCs.

Engaging Communities in Teacher Education Programs

In the last two decades, some teacher educators and scholars who have been focused on including communities in teacher education programs have rejected the idea of limiting community participation to involving families and communities as passive reactors to work that teacher education programs have already done or as guest speakers in courses where everything has already been framed for them. Instead, they have sought ways to engage community members at the beginning in the conceptualization, development, and planning of classes, seminars, and other program-learning experiences for TCs. Here there is an attempt to level the traditional power-knowledge hierarchy away from one where university knowledge is treated as more important than community knowledge (Clark, Zygmunt, Tancock, & Cipollone, 2021; Hyland & Meacham, 2004; Zeichner, Bowman, Guillen, & Napolitan, 2016). The participation of community members in co-teaching or co-planning a class session or a learning activity, by itself, does not indicate whose knowledge counts in the collaboration process. This all depends on the nature and quality of the relations that are developed between the program teacher educators and their community collaborators.

The Illinois State University's *Chicago Teacher Education Pipeline* is one example of a teacher preparation program that shifted the power by including the genuine and reciprocal engagement of community participants in conceptualizing planning and implementing community-centered activities in a TPP (Mustian, O'Mally, Garcia, Millan, & Zamudio-Mainou, 2021). Here community members are involved from the beginning of the process.

> One of the keys to our partnership has been the inclusion and integration of community voices in the design and delivery of every aspect of our urban teacher preparation work. Community experiences cannot just be added on as a stand-alone experience and community knowledge must be honored and compensated. (p. 96)[4]

This inclusion of community influence in the conceptualization and planning of learning experiences for teacher candidates was also often the case in the University Washington program noted earlier when three of the community activists who served as coordinators of the community component of the programs recruited additional community mentors for specific activities in the program and met with university teacher educators to decide together what topics would be addressed at particular sessions and how the sessions would be structured. They also decided which community members would be best for participating in particular sessions and recruited, prepared, and supported the community mentors in their interactions with teacher candidates. Finally, they also regularly participated in the preparation and debriefing of teacher candidates' sessions with community mentors and led the effort to establish a system for compensating mentors for the work that they did with teacher candidates (Guillen & Zeichner, 2018; Napolitan et al., 2019; Zeichner, Bowman, Guillen, & Napolitan, 2016).

Teacher Education Programs and Communities Working in Solidarity

Even when there is genuine community engagement in teacher preparation programs, the focus is often on issues of teacher preparation (how community participants can help programs prepare better teachers) and not on other issues of concern to communities in education and in the social, economic, and political contexts surrounding education. Working in solidarity with communities means that there also needs to be a focus on how teacher educators can support efforts by community members to address inequitable opportunities related to things like inequities in educational funding and school discipline policies; disparities in housing, healthcare, transportation, and policing; access to nutritious food, and the availability of work that pays a living wage. Teacher education and community partnerships have often represented an extractive approach to communities where the focus is mainly on what communities can do for teacher educators to help prepare successful teachers. Less common have been partnerships that are based on a commitment to mutual benefit for both the TPPs and the communities (Mule, 2010). Working in solidarity with communities requires attention to the issue of benefits for the communities and reflects a concern for both educational justice and community well-being from the perspectives of community members (Ishimaru, 2019).

One example of teachers working in solidarity with communities is the recent synergy that has developed in the United States between several local teacher unions practicing what they define as "social justice unionism" (Peterson, 1999) and community-based organizing efforts. Social justice unionism is a model for what teacher educators could be doing and is a powerful way for unions and communities to join together in shared interest to advocate for changes in schooling and in the social and economic conditions affecting it that further the goal of greater equity. A key priority of social justice teacher unionism according to Peterson (1999) is "building coalitions and alliances with parent and community advocacy groups that speak to both school reform and ensuring equity in the society as a whole" (p. 19). In recent years, teacher strikes in cities like LA, Chicago, and Seattle have reflected a social justice approach to unionism where what teachers bargained for and won went beyond the classic trade and professional union approaches of focusing solely on salaries, benefits, and working conditions for teachers. For example, in the 2015 teacher strike in Seattle, teachers won several things that were also desired by parents such as thirty minutes of recess daily for all elementary students, a one-year ban on the suspension of elementary students for non-violent offenses, and the creation of task forces in thirty schools to examine equity issues including disciplinary ones that have disproportionally affected BIPOC students (Strauss, 2015).[5]

There have been many examples in recent years of local community-initiated efforts to address the systemic racial, economic, and educational inequities that impact the lives of students and their families in nondominant communities. Some of these efforts have involved collaborations between teachers, teacher unions, and community organizers, parents, families, and students and have linked educational reform to community revitalization (e.g., Anyon, 2014; Orr & Rogers, 2011; Warren & Mapp, 2011; Warren & Goodman, 2018).

There has also been an extension of the kind of work involved in social justice teacher unionism to issues of teacher preparation. Here some individual teacher educators have joined or formed alliances with existing local social movements, and organizations working for greater racial, economic, political, and educational justice in nondominant communities. These teacher educators have worked alongside and visibly supported community organizers, parents/caregivers, and community leaders to address the broad range of issues and inequities that affect nondominant communities including in education.

So far, there have been few visible examples of teacher education programs that have broadened their work to include advocating and supporting community organizing efforts to work for broader equity in nondominant communities beyond issues of teacher preparation. For example, there have been many instances of individual teacher educators becoming involved in community-initiated efforts to address problems in education, housing, transportation, access to clean air and water and nutritious food, and in collaborating with communities to work against such problems as school segregation, inequitable school funding and staffing, the defunding of public schools, and discriminatory discipline policies. However, there have not been many programmatic efforts in teacher education programs where program faculty and students join forces with community advocacy groups to work on issues that were initiated by communities.

One example of an individual teacher educator collaborating with a community to address a broader community concern is when Indiana University teacher educator Marilynn Boyle-Baise (Boyle-Baise, 2005) and her teacher candidates assisted a local African American community in compiling an oral history of the Benjamin Banneker school that served African American students from 1915 to 1951 through interviews with surviving former students.

An example of program activism with communities in support of social justice goals is the work of teacher educators and teacher candidates at Ball State University in helping the local African American community with which they partner for teacher preparation to develop and distribute a community-identified canon of children's literature (Tancock, Zygmunt, Clark, Clausen, & Mucherah, 2017), to develop a neighborhood civil rights museum privileging historical and contemporary local social justice victories (Zygmunt & Cipollone, 2018) and to help fundraise for the restoration of a historic neighborhood church (Zygmunt & Cipollone, 2018).

An example of program activism with communities in support of social justice goals that are linked to ongoing community struggles for justice is the work of UCLA Center X teacher education faculty over the last thirty years in preparing teachers and educational leaders in programs that work closely with educators and community activists in LA to challenge policies and practices in education and beyond that undermine the dignity and opportunities for families in these communities (Francois & Hunter Quartz, 2021). One example of Center X teacher educators working alongside LA educators, students, and community activists in this regard was a 2017 gathering at Roosevelt High School in East LA[6] that included educators and students in LA Unified School District, UCLA teacher and leader candidates, and Center X educators right at the beginning of Trump's presidency when he launched attacks on immigrants and refugees in the United States from certain countries.

A final example of a teacher education program responding to issues initiated by community members and working alongside communities to address them is related work at the University of Washington in Seattle (UW). This initiative is related to supporting Washington tribal communities' efforts to help teachers and teacher candidates learn about the history and cultures of the thirty-two tribal nations that reside within the geographical area of the state and how to teach Indigenous students in more culturally responsive and sustaining ways.

When I began working at the UW as the director of teacher education in 2009, I joined a "study group" that had been established a few years before that involved several members of the College of Education faculty including teacher education faculty, American Indian Studies program faculty, tribal leaders and tribal educators from across the state including an Indigenous elder who was a member of the state legislature. One focus of the discussions in this group over several years was the reactions of the Indigenous communities in the state to the quality of the educators that were being prepared in the UW's professional education programs to work with Native students. These discussions with community members included meetings with tribal leaders and tribal educators that focused exclusively on the quality of our teacher education programs with regard to Indigenous communities in the state. During these meetings, we received consistent feedback that graduates from our teacher preparation programs did not understand Indigenous students or their communities, and that we were not doing much to help prepare more Indigenous teachers.

Continued conversations about these issues over a period of a few years led to a collaboration between UW teacher educators and Native American leaders and educators. First, an optional and relatively new statewide school curriculum developed by Indigenous educators and leaders in Washington called *Since Time Immemorial: Tribal Sovereignty in Washington State* was integrated into the curriculum of UW teacher education programs before it became a state requirement for teacher education programs and for K-12 public schools to use it.[7] Additionally, a Native Education Certificate program was jointly developed by tribal members and university teacher educators that prepares educators throughout the state to work with Indigenous students in culturally responsive and sustaining ways. The courses in this program are

Designed to cultivate the educator's ability to create meaningful and effective relationships with Native American students through a perspective of being a community-based teacher. Educators will develop the expertise of engaging Native students, families, and communities in instruction to ensure Native students thrive and succeed making school and future careers relevant to the pressing needs of Native communities.[8]

In addition, all teacher candidates from all five of UW's teacher education programs complete a course in the Native Education Certificate program as part of their initial certification program and many teachers around the state have completed part or all of the program.

The Nature and Quality of Community Experiences for Teacher Candidates

Length and Depth of Community Experiences

Nondominant communities have served as sites for teacher learning for teacher candidates in many different ways that vary in the length and depth of experience and in terms of what teacher candidates are expected to do while in the community. In terms of length, the experiences have ranged from very brief "dips" into a community to complete a community study or visit a community-based organization to learn about its work to long-term cultural immersion experiences in programs like the Teacher Corps that last for one to two years and/or include living with families in the community as in the case of the Chicago Teacher Education Pipeline (Lee, 2018; Mustian, O'Mally, Garcia, Millan, & Zamudio-Mainou, 2021) and the Teachers for Alaska program, a program that prepared teachers to teach in remote rural villages often only accessible by a small airplane (Noordhoff & Kleinfeld, 1993).

Activities and Settings in Community Experiences

Teacher candidates who participate in community experiences during their programs have engaged in a variety of different kinds of activities including going on community walks or bus tours guided by either faculty or community members and sometimes students, completing a community study to better understand some aspects and needs of a community, mapping the resources within a community, tutoring, mentoring, or coaching kids connected to a program in a community-based organization or religious institution, participating in community cultural events, helping with family chores as part of a homestay, coaching a community athletic team, and listening to community members talk about their feelings about their neighborhood schools. Some programs require teacher candidates to meet with the families of their students either by visiting them at their homes or at some other mutually agreeable location such as a coffee shop or park. Examples of the different kinds of interactions that TCs have engaged in during community experiences in their programs will be discussed in the next chapter. These examples will illustrate the impact that particular versions of these community-based activities have had on the learning and development of prospective teachers, as well as some of the complexities that are involved in the use of these practices.

Schools as Settings for Community Experiences

Although many community experiences in teacher education programs are situated in local community organizations, not all community experiences take place outside of school settings. There are two main types of school settings that have provided community experiences for prospective teachers: (1) public community schools and (2) schools set up by community members and educators to supplement what students receive in their regular public school. Public community schools, like the one in which I taught that was described in the Preface, include some form of collaborative governance by parents/caregivers, community members, and educators and represent a set of partnerships between school and other community resources that serve both youth and adults (Oakes, Franke, Quartz, & Rogers, 2006).[9] Teacher candidates who complete their clinical placements in a public community school often have frequent contact with the family members of students and other community members, and learn to teach in an environment in which all staff see their responsibilities to the whole community served by their school in addition to their responsibilities to their students.[10]

Community Experiences in a Public Community School: Fratney School/La Escuela Fratney

In 1988, a group of parents community activists, and teachers in a multiracial neighborhood in Milwaukee Wisconsin won approval from their school district to use a vacant school building in their neighborhood to start a new public community school that would take advantage of the cultural strengths and resources in their community. La Escuela Fratney[11] opened later that year as a two-way bilingual school where all students[12] were educated in both Spanish and English. The school was designated as one with site-based management, and parents/caregivers and teachers had substantive involvement in major decisions concerning the school. During the years when I was a teacher educator at the University of Wisconsin, we placed several student teachers each year at this school under the guidance of mentor teachers, many of whom were affiliated with *Rethinking Schools*,[13] a group of education and community activists who advocate for greater racial and educational justice in public education. The teacher candidates who were assigned to this school typically became involved in the Rethinking Schools group and developed an awareness of community perspectives on education and other issues to a much greater extent than those in typical school placements.

Community Experiences in a Private Community-Based School: The African American Ethnic Academy

Sometimes members of a community (e.g., linked to particular community-based organizations or religious organizations) develop and provide educational services to students in a particular community that are intended to supplement the education students receive in public schools (also see Jackson, 2006). In 1994, a group of African American teachers in the

Madison Wisconsin school district, together with community members, started a half-day Saturday program for African American students with the goal of hopefully reducing some of the gaps that existed between African American and other students in the district. The program (The African American Academy) was based on a locally developed framework of culturally responsive teaching focused on the African American experience, and served about 125 students a year from pre-K through eighth grade during its fourteen years of existence. The instructors in the program were Madison district teachers, University of Wisconsin-Madison teacher candidates, family members of students who attended the school, and other community members. Many teacher candidates in the elementary teacher education program volunteered at this school as part of their community experience requirement in their program.

One of the most important components of the Academy's program was *Harambee*[14] time which occurred at the beginning and end of every day. During Harambe time, students and teachers affirmed their dreams and ambitions and their pride in being African Americans. Another important event at the school was the annual *Kwanzaa*[15] celebration which occurred every December. It was an opportunity for students to showcase, to family and community members, what they learned in the program during the fall term. The curriculum in the Academy connected the academic content to the African American experience. One example of this was in a science and social studies lesson where a teacher explained to her students how Harriet Tubman used the stars to guide herself and the slaves she was helping escape slavery, on their way to the North and freedom during the US Civil War in the nineteenth century.

According to the co-directors of the program "We pounded our hearts and souls into making sure that the kids could see themselves in the curriculum."[16] Also, some of the policies common in schools were not allowed in the Academy such as putting kids out into the hallways when they acted out in the classroom. Volunteers had to find ways to deal with student disruptions that kept them in the classroom

Student teachers and other teacher candidates who were at the earlier stages of their two-year program volunteered at the Academy, and some continued volunteering even after they completed the program. According to one of the directors of the program:

> Many of them stayed with us for a number of years . . . They just got stronger and stronger and began to understand some of the things and how we did them culturally that looked quite different than what they were experiencing in a school setting . . . They also got to see students in different settings because many of the students they taught in the Academy also attended schools where they taught.[17]

My teacher education colleagues and I, as well as the Academy staff, noticed that participation in the Academy over time seemed to have a big impact on the teacher candidates' teaching. Recently, one of the co-directors of the program described to me how several student teachers of different racial backgrounds, who had volunteered in the Academy for several years before becoming teachers in the Madison schools, were introducing many of the culturally responsive teaching practices learned at the Academy into their classrooms.

She also described a White teacher who had gone on to become an award-winning teacher and education adviser to President Barack Obama. He also became a school principal and brought the practices that he learned in the Academy into his school. For example:

> He took almost everything he learned from the Academy and incorporated it into a school. So you would walk into the school in the morning, a diverse school, and you would hear affirmations, you would hear the chants that we would do at the academy, and you would see cultural imaging . . . He just recently built a whole schoolwide curriculum where murals were being painted throughout the whole school inside and out called "I am somebody." He created

a council of elders at the school where family members and community members had a say in what was going to happen in the school. And he borrowed from some of the ways that African tribes are set up so the parents instead of having a traditional parent-teacher organization role, were part of a council of elders.[18]

The teacher candidates who volunteered in the program were not assigned individual teacher mentors but were instead mentored as part of the entire group of teachers and volunteers who regularly debriefed and analyzed their work with students.

Links between Community Experiences and Programs

Community experiences for teacher candidates always stand in some relation to the rest of a teacher preparation program. The most common experience seems to be that community experiences, if and when they are part of teacher candidates' learning-to-teach experiences, are very weakly connected to the rest of a teacher preparation program. For example, the Urban Education program of the Associated Colleges of the Midwest included one or two student teaching experiences complemented by various seminars and other community activities during a term or an academic year, but these were mostly unconnected to the rest of the teacher education programs in the liberal arts colleges that sent teacher candidates to the program for their student teaching semester or year (Zeichner & Melnick, 1996b). This has also been true for Indiana University's Navajo Nation Project that includes a semester to a year immersion and student teaching plus interactions with the program staff on the reservation and at the university. While there is a year-long orientation for this program carried out by program faculty with readings and assignments, there are not strong links to the teacher candidates' home teacher preparation programs either at Indiana University or the other colleges and universities that supply participants to this community immersion and student teaching program (Zeichner & Melnick, 1996a).

In other cases, links have been established between specific coursework and community experiences. In the most common form of these examples, community experiences for teacher candidates have been incorporated into individual program courses where the candidates complete assignments in their community placement related to the course content such as Haddix's (2015) requirement in her secondary literacy methods course at Syracuse University that engages teacher candidates in a community writing project. Other examples include a community study project carried out in connection with a specific course in Vietnam (Nguyen & Zeichner, 2021), in South Africa (Ramsaroop & Peterson, 2020), and in Hong Kong (Harfitt & Chow, 2018).

Less commonly, there have been links between community experiences and a few other program courses such as what exists in Ball State University's "Schools within the Context of Community" semester in its elementary program where teacher candidates complete several courses that are based in the community (Zygmunt & Clark, 2016; Clark, Zygmunt, Tancock, & Cipollone, 2021). This link of community experience with multiple courses also existed at the University of Washington where in the first phase of this work elementary teacher candidates spent two half-days per week working in a service-oriented community-based organization (CBO). Several course instructors in the program during the period of time that the teacher candidates participated in these community experiences negotiated their course assignments with the organization directors if an assignment was to be completed during teacher candidates' work in the organization (Brayko, 2013; McDonald et al., 2013).

A few years later at the University of Washington, in the second phase of the work, the program evolved to include a greater variety of community experiences and interactions with community mentors on campus and in communities. At this point, a community strand was structured into courses during several terms of the year-long program in the elementary and secondary education programs including in student teaching (Guillen & Zeichner, 2018; Zeichner, Bowman, Guillen, & Napolitan, 2016).

Mostly though, the trajectory of community experience in teacher education has followed the same pattern that multicultural education did in its early years in teacher education programs in the United States (Ladson-Billings, 1995) where the community dimensions of a program exist in isolation within individual courses with weak connections to the rest of the program (Harfitt, 2019). Haddix (2015) has stressed the importance of linking community experiences such as service learning to coursework so that programs can avoid strengthening and reinforcing the deficit-oriented stereotypes that TCs often bring to these experiences about the communities they enter.

> Opportunities for preservice teachers to participate in service learning within urban school communities can further reify perspectives and ideologies if these opportunities are not coordinated alongside coursework and teacher education classroom experiences where teacher educators and preservice teachers do the required and necessary work of critical thinking, questioning and dialoging about what is learned from working with communities. (Haddix, 2015, p. 66)

There are many complicating factors involved in managing both school and community placements such as when school-based clinical experiences are coupled with community-based experiences during the same term (Gallego, 2001). Here sometimes a conflict arises between what is the best site for teacher candidate learning for each placement. For example, when I started working at UW in 2009, there was a requirement in one program for elementary teacher candidates to spend three half-days in a school placement linked to three methods courses and to also spend another two half-days at a community-based placement linked to a seminar. In some cases teacher candidates had been assigned to a CBO that was utilized by students in their school and were able to observe and work with students at their school in two different learning environments. In other cases, community placements were made in another neighborhood based on what teacher educators thought would offer the best learning experience for teacher candidates. The teacher candidates who were able to complete both placements in a particular community typically found their experiences more valuable than those candidates who completed their community placement in another community. Candidates whose community placement was in a neighborhood different than the ones served by their school often spent a lot of time driving from one site to the other (McDonald, Bowman, and Brayko, 2013). This example illustrates the complexity that is always present in setting up and managing community-based experiences in programs where there are multiple and sometimes competing needs.

The Stance of Teacher Candidates and/or Teacher Educators Toward Communities

Another important aspect of community experiences is the stance assumed by teacher candidates and teacher educators who participate in these experiences toward the communities which they enter including their purposes for doing so. It has been very common for deficit views of nondominant communities to be present among teacher candidates even in programs that describe themselves as social justice programs (Zeichner, 2019b). For example, many teacher candidates see their purpose in teaching in these communities to educating kids to be successful in school so that they can eventually leave their communities. These "missionary" perspectives reflect a view of trying to "save" students from their allegedly broken communities and are sometimes strengthened and reinforced in efforts by teacher educators to help teacher candidates become more familiar with communities in ways that do not involve interacting and developing relationships with community members and learning from them. An example of this is when teacher candidates are asked to complete a map of a community's resources with only minimal interactions with people who live in a community) (See Barnes, 2017, 2020 and Jackson and Bryson (2018) for a discussion of this problem). This view of "teacher as savior" stands in contrast with instances where teacher candidates see themselves primarily as learners in the community, and they recognize and want to access the expertise and cultural wealth of families and community members so that they can do their work better (e.g., Zygmunt et al. (2018).

I do not intend to suggest here that the stance of teacher candidates toward communities—and therefore toward their community field experiences—is a fixed entity. On the contrary, as will be discussed in the next chapter, research has clearly shown there are certain design and pedagogical features of community experiences such as the nature and quality of mentoring and mediation by teacher educators that can be utilized to help change these missionary orientations to ones that are more asset-oriented (e.g., Seidl & Friend, 2002; Sleeter, 2008).

Preparing Homegrown Teachers in Nondominant Communities

In some cases, teacher education programs have partnered with local school districts and CBOs in nondominant communities to design special teacher education programs to recruit and prepare teachers from nondominant communities to teach in these communities over time (e.g., Heller, 2021). Oftentimes, community-based Grow Your Own programs are developed because of community frustration with the quality of teaching provided by largely White middle-class beginning teachers whom they believe have little knowledge of their kids and communities and see their mission as one of saving kids from their allegedly dysfunctional communities. As Warren (2011) points out, GYO programs[19] are premised on the idea that "community members who become teachers will practice differently and better because of their deep connections to students and their families" (p. 40). The efforts in GYO programs to recruit more teachers of color into nondominant communities are supported by much research that shows the positive effects of students being taught by teachers who look like them and the benefits of BIPOC teachers for all students. Summaries of some of the research that underlines the importance of achieving greater diversity in the teaching force can be found in Carver-Thomas, 2018; Klopfenstein, 2005; Villegas & Irvine, 2010; Will 2014.

For many years, there has been a serious problem of teacher attrition from schools in nondominant communities. This has resulted in a disproportionate number of inexperienced teachers teaching in these schools as well as the problem of teachers teaching outside of their fields of certification (National Academies of Sciences, Engineering, and Medicine, 2020). This situation has negatively impacted learning opportunities and outcomes for students in these schools (e.g., Cardichon, Darling-Hammond, Yang, Shields, & Burns, 2020; Sorenson & Ladd, 2020). Community-based GYO programs have the potential to reduce this teacher attrition and provide greater access to experienced and fully prepared teachers to students in nondominant communities.

GYO programs are varied in their structures and in terms of who they attempt to recruit into teaching. Many of these programs focus on recruiting and preparing BIPOC teachers who are underrepresented in the teaching force, sometimes focusing on specific groups of individuals such as males of color.[20] According to Gist, Bianco, and Lynn (2017), some programs focus on developing an interest among middle and high school students to develop an interest in becoming teachers. Recruitment in community-based and often community-driven GYO programs typically focuses on: "adult members of the local school and geographic community such as paraprofessionals, school cafeteria workers, crossing and security guards, and custodial staff as well as parents, community activists, and religious leaders" (p. 3).

One prominent example of a community-driven and community-based GYO program is the one in Chicago that emerged out of efforts initiated by the Logan Square neighborhood association (LSNA) in northwest Chicago to find a way to enable a largely immigrant population (mostly women as well as a small number of men) who were participating in a parent mentoring program in their neighborhood schools to become certified teachers. Initially, LSNA formed a partnership with Chicago State University to prepare some of the parent mentors (Hong, 2011) to become bilingual teachers. This program later evolved into a broader partnership with Northeastern Illinois University and Chicago Public Schools to prepare individuals from the Logan Square community to become teachers in their community (e.g., Skinner, Garreton, & Schultz, 2011; VanWinkle, 2017). This then evolved into a statewide network of GYO programs in communities throughout Illinois (VanWinkle, 2017).

In addition to community-driven and community-based GYO programs that prepare teachers from specific nondominant communities to teach in their communities, there is the more specific case of Indigenous teacher education programs that prepare Indigenous teachers, and in some cases, also prepare non-Indigenous teachers, to be better teachers for Indigenous students by learning about Indigenous cultures, histories, and contemporary circumstances. Indigenous teacher education programs currently exist in several countries in addition to the United States including Australia, Canada, and Aotearoa New Zealand (e.g., Haig-Brown & Kawehau Hoskins, 2019; Reid, 2004; Whitinuip, Rodriguez de Francem, & Mclvor, 2018).

One of the central features of Indigenous teacher education programs is Indigenous control even when the programs are embedded in partnerships with teacher education faculties in universities. For example, one of the most prominent of these programs is the Indigenous Teacher Education Program in British Columbia, Canada (NITEP) which is a partnership that began in 1974 between the University of British Columbia and The First Nations Educational Council comprised of representatives from communities where the regional field centers are located including tribal elders, program graduates, professional education associations, and the Associate Deans for teacher education and Indigenous education at UBC. According to Archibald (2008, 2015), who directed the program for many years, Indigenous people have been centrally involved in the planning of the program and throughout its ongoing development "the program is an Indian idea, is Indian controlled, and its philosophy is Indian, although the program falls under the jurisdiction of the University of British Columbia" (p. 15).

Another example of a community-driven and community-based GYO program in the United States is the *Indigenous Roots Teacher Education Program (ROOTS)* in Nebraska.[21] This four-year federally funded program which has been in existence for over twenty years is a partnership between the Little Priest Tribal College, the University of Nebraska Lincoln College of Education and Human Sciences, The Nebraska Department of Education, and currently four Indigenous communities in Nebraska. The program prepares Indigenous paraprofessionals to be elementary and bilingual teachers in Nebraska tribal schools in four communities. Like the Native Indian Teacher Education program in Canada, the Indigenous communities involved are genuinely engaged in decisions about the substance of the program including making decisions about which applicants will be admitted (Heller, 2021).

Conclusion

As is often the case with the use of frameworks that purport to portray the dimensions of variation in ambiguous concepts like community, understanding the different meanings of the term community in teacher education programs is understandably more complicated than any simple classification system may suggest. Programs contain examples of both community involvement and engagement in different courses or clinical experiences, and teacher educators and community members often work together in different ways over time as personnel change and grants expire. Additionally, teacher education programs exist in institutional environments that vary in their support for the incorporation of communities into the preparation of teachers.

Another element of complexity in understanding community experiences and community participation in teacher education programs is that the type of community experience for teacher candidates or the type of participation in a teacher preparation program by community members is not determinative of the relationships of power and knowledge that exist or the attitudes of teacher candidates and teacher educators toward particular communities. For example, guest speaking in a TPP class or serving on an advisory committee and reacting to aspects of an existing TPP does not necessarily mean that community input into a TPP is limited to involvement. Nor does appointing community members to a staff position in a program necessarily mean that they are able to assert the agency to conceptualize, develop, and implement a course in their preferred ways. The key element to involvement or engagement or working in solidarity is the ways in which knowledge and power operate over time in the relationships between community members and other school and university/ program staff who participate in the partnerships.

Similarly, when teacher candidates engage in particular types of activities during community experiences such as tutoring a child in an after school program or attending a Sunday church service the type of experience, in and of itself, does not develop or bolster an asset-based perspective toward the communities in which they complete their experiences or determine whether an asset-based stance toward a community develops during the experience, or, if it does develop, whether it persists afterward. Other factors such as the nature and quality of preparation for and mediation of the experience and its connection to the rest of the preparation program deeply influence the impact of a community experience on teacher candidates. Furthermore, the ability of teacher candidates to incorporate their learning from community experiences into culturally responsive and sustaining curriculum and instruction in their classrooms cannot be taken for granted and depends on a variety of factors beyond the experience itself.

A final example of how it is not merely the type of activity that determines its influence on teacher candidates, but the way in which power has been exercised in developing and implementing it (e.g., whose perspectives are represented in these processes), comes from a research study that I was involved in in the 1990s. In this project, my colleague Susan Melnick and I conducted a study of three teacher education programs that utilized cultural immersion in nondominant communities and extensive instruction of teacher candidates by community residents and elders as central features in educating teachers to become community teachers. Part of our research including visiting each program for at least a week and interviewing and observing teacher candidates, teacher educators, and community-based mentors. During our visit to one of these programs, the *Teachers for Alaska* program, which prepared teachers (many of them from outside Alaska) to teach in schools in remote rural Indigenous villages (Noordhoff & Kleinfeld, 1993), I remember being excited about the case studies of each community that candidates read and discussed in their classes. I thought that it was a great idea to construct these cases as one way to orient candidates to the communities they would be living and learning to teach in for the year.

The one thing about this visit that I remember to this day is that when an Indigenous teacher educator who taught some of the courses in the program overheard me say something to someone on our research team about the cases, he pulled me aside and began to tell me that although he thought it was a good idea to have cases for each of the host communities, he felt that there was not enough community input into what went into the cases and how they were developed. He then went on to give me examples of some of the ways the cases would have been different had community members played a more central role in their development. Although I no longer remember the specifics of how the cases would have been different with greater community control over their development, from then on, I began to pay more attention to the question of whose knowledge and whose perspectives are represented in programs that seek to educate teachers for schools in nondominant communities.

In the next chapter, I examine what research on community participation in teacher education programs and community experiences for teacher candidates suggests influences the impact that communities have on both programs and teacher candidates. A set of design principles is proposed based on existing research that suggests which features of engagement with communities in teacher education should be present in the work in order to support the development of community teachers who are willing and able to teach in more culturally and community responsive and sustaining ways.

CHAPTER FOUR

Creating the Conditions in Teacher Education Programs for Preparing Community-Focused Culturally Responsive and Sustaining Teachers

In this chapter, I discuss several design principles based on existing research, including those studies conducted by teacher educators who have critically reflected on their attempts to connect their courses and/or programs more closely to the expertise and resources in the nondominant communities in which their students learn to teach. These design elements describe the features of working with local communities in teacher preparation programs that seem to be important in achieving the qualities of partnerships with communities that support the preparation of teachers who are willing and able to build on the funds of knowledge and community cultural wealth in their students' families and communities. Following the discussion of these principles, I discuss several strategies for creating the conditions in teacher education that I believe will make it more likely that these elements will be able to exist and be sustained in programs over time. Underlying this discussion is the assumption that in order to have teacher preparation programs that are successful in preparing culturally responsive and sustaining teachers, we must have *community-engaged teacher educators* who model the practices they encourage their students to use in their classrooms.

It should be acknowledged that there is limited systematic research available in the United States and internationally that has shown causality on issues related to how to effectively prepare teachers to engage with families, individuals, and organizations in nondominant communities (e.g., Mancenido & Pello, 2020). This being said, consistent peer-reviewed research does exist related to community engagement in teacher education, the broader field of multicultural teacher education, and specifically with regard to the preparation of teachers to teach in culturally responsive and sustaining ways. This research collectively suggests which practices are more likely to reproduce and possibly even strengthen deficit perspectives among teacher candidates about students and their families and communities and which practices are more likely to succeed in providing both teacher educators and teacher candidates with access to the family and community expertise and resources that can help teacher candidates provide an education more likely to help students see their lives outside of school reflected in their education in school (e.g., Carter & Darling-Hammond, 2016; Cochran-Smith & Villegas, 2016).

Design Principles for Working with Communities in Teacher Education

Starting with the Teacher Educators

The first aspect of teacher preparation programs that must be addressed for community engagement in teacher education to succeed in preparing culturally responsive and sustaining teachers for schools in nondominant communities is to start with the teacher educators. Much of the literature on communities in teacher education focuses exclusively on teacher candidates and implies that teacher educators have the knowledge, skills, experience, will, and capacity to do this work successfully and that it is only necessary to focus on the teacher candidates. However, the reality is that like many teachers and teacher candidates, many teacher educators bring little personal experience to their roles in living and/or working in nondominant communities like the ones in which their teacher candidates are prepared to teach, and they often gain little knowledge of the communities in which their teacher candidates' complete their clinical work. One consequence of this lack of knowledge of the communities, and often the schools as well, in which students complete their clinical experiences is that coursework is often viewed by teacher candidates as not relevant to the situations in which they are learning to teach (Zeichner, 2010).

It is argued by some scholars who have studied work with communities in teacher education programs that teacher candidates should see community-centered work modeled by their teacher educators both in their teacher education coursework and in their clinical experiences in schools (e.g., Haddix, 2015; Hyland & Meacham, 2004). However, one of the endemic problems in teacher education programs has been the gap between what teacher educators tell their teacher candidates to do in their classrooms and what they do in their own teacher education classrooms. This contradiction with regard to culturally responsive and sustaining teaching has weakened the impact of teacher educators' messages on their teacher candidates' beliefs and practices about the importance of engaging with communities (Kretchmar & Zeichner, 2016).

One example of this prevalent contradiction between the words and actions of teacher educators in the United States has been the widespread talk by teacher educators about the importance of preparing teachers to teach in culturally responsive and sustaining ways while not addressing in their own teaching the varied experiences and backgrounds of their own teacher candidates. Many preparation programs that serve predominantly White and monolingual English-speaking candidates are primarily geared toward the White English-speaking candidates who have enrolled in them. It is clear that many BIPOC teacher candidates who often bring very different kinds of experiences than White students to their programs have expressed their frustration with the neglect of their own experiences and needs in preparing to be teachers (e.g., Kohli, 2021).

In the United States, 70 percent of teacher candidates are White as are 87 percent of adjunct instructors and 91 percent of tenure-track instructors in teacher preparation programs (Kohli, & Pizarro, 2022). In addition to the focus of curriculum and instruction in many programs on the preparation of White teachers to teach in minoritized communities, it has been asserted by some scholars that programs often "embody and condone deficit framings" (Kohli & Pizarro, 2022, p. 8) of BIPOC students and their communities. Brown (2014) has asserted that many BIPOC teacher candidates have felt isolated and alienated in their programs that they have felt were dominated by a White lens and not interested in learning about and building on their own lived experiences and social and cultural knowledge.

There are several things that can be done to help teacher educators learn to model the culturally responsive and sustaining teaching that they often urge their teacher candidates to use in their classrooms such as preparing and hiring a more diverse group of teacher educators so that the demographics of those who prepare teachers reflects a wider range of experiences and cultural perspectives than currently (Goodwin, 2004). Another important action that teacher education institutions should take is to help teacher educators gain a better understanding of the resources and perspectives in the nondominant communities in which they are preparing teacher candidates to teach in ways where both the teacher educators and community members learn more about each other and avoid the common situation of one-way gazing from the academy into the community (Cross, 2005; Lees, 2016).

There are several ways in which teacher educators have attempted to become more knowledgeable about the nondominant communities in which their teacher candidates teach during their preparation for teaching and to broaden the focus of their work to reflect the diverse backgrounds of teacher candidates and the communities in which they learn to teach. Probably the most common way that this has happened is that individual teacher educators, sometimes together with a few colleagues, develop relationships with local community activists, CBOs, or local religious establishments and work with these community partners to develop a community engagement or service learning component in one or more of their courses where candidates' work in their courses is connected to their activities in the community.

One example of this in practice is the work of literacy teacher educator Marcelle Haddix (2015) at Syracuse University who developed community links in her literacy methods course. Haddix (2015) believes that there is a danger that community experiences for teacher candidates such as service learning experiences can, without careful mediation and critical reflection, dialogue, and questioning about what is learned from working in and with communities, further reify the deficit perspectives that novices often bring to these experiences and strengthen and reinforce the missionary zeal that is displayed by many teacher candidates.

Haddix (2015) believes that in order to do genuine community engagement work in teacher education programs, teacher educators have to assume the role of community-engaged teacher educators:

> I have to embody and practice what I preach. It is not enough for me to merely encourage students to go out and

work with communities or to coordinate opportunities for them to participate in service learning. . . . My model of community-engaged teaching starts first with my own work as a community-engaged teacher educator and scholar. (p. 67)

Haddix (2015) initiated a community-based writing conference that she framed as community engagement rather than service learning ("Writing for Our Lives") to support the writing practices of local middle and high school youth in their local communities, and she also has held workshops at local CBOs and public libraries. Candidates in her writing methods class develop and facilitate workshops for the conference, and they attend and participate in writing events in the local community as a part of their requirements for the course. Haddix (2015) argues that one of her goals in this work is to help her "students understand their roles as teachers within a school community context and to bridge what is happening within their classrooms with the broader local and global communities" (p. 68).

Another way in which teacher educators have become engaged with the communities in which their students learn to teach is when program leaders or Deans organize and then encourage or require teacher educators to engage with community members in relation to the task of educating teachers for their communities. There are several examples in the literature of programs where teacher educators were required and/or supported to spend time learning about the communities in which their students were learning to teach and to revise their courses and programs to make them more relevant to these contexts. One example of this work was briefly mentioned earlier where faculty at Illinois State University who teach courses in the Chicago Teacher Education Pipeline program are required to participate in immersion experiences in the program's partner neighborhoods in Chicago and two nearby cities. Faculty are provided by the program with places to stay in the communities, and the school and community partners who work with the teacher candidates educate the teacher educators about their neighborhoods and schools (Mustian, O'Mally, Garcia; Millan, & Zamudio-Mainou, 2021).

> Faculty "live" in Chicago for 5 days and visit Peoria and Decatur for 1 day each, where they learn about each community from community members. They spend time in partner schools, visit various community assets, and engage in meaningful dialogue with various stakeholders (e.g., families, teachers, community leaders). Though many of our affiliated faculty who go through this professional learning process have been connected to urban communities in some way, we are intentional that each community is unique and must be known by faculty before they can even begin to prepare teacher candidates to understand the sociocultural contexts integrated into urban redeveloped courses. (p. 65)

Stakeholders from the partner communities work with faculty in the redesign and development of new courses and other experiences to help make them more relevant to the preparation of teachers for their communities (e.g., see Lee, 2018; Mustian, Lee, Nelson, Gamboa-Turner, & Roule, 2017). Community-based teacher educators are compensated for their work in educating faculty about their communities, participating in the redesign of courses, and for working directly with teacher candidates.

In another example in Chicago involving Teacher Educators at Northeastern Illinois University, the Education Dean organized "community study days" over several years for faculty to meet with community partners. Here, faculty met with students, school staff, family and community members, and activists. In these meetings, faculty learned more about issues pertinent to the neighborhoods and their schools such as housing foreclosures, access to healthcare, the arts, and they examined the implications of these social issues for the

schools in the community (Gillette, 2011). Faculty also met
with parents and teachers in the development of annual school
improvement plans that each school was required to construct.

Based on these community study days and other
collaborations with community partners:

> Some faculty members completely revamped the types of
> readings, course materials, and assessments they used. . . .
> Faculty members began to select material for courses that
> could serve two purposes: teach content or strategy and
> incorporate the lived realities of urban students. . . . Faculty
> began to make programmatic changes that were influenced
> by our community work including completely restructuring
> the type of general education coursework that all candidates
> received. (Gillette, 2018, p. 124)

In another example, the teacher education faculty at the
University of Massachusetts-Boston (Koerner & Abdul-
Tawwab, 2006) conducted an assessment of how well they
were preparing urban teachers and concluded that there was
"an almost complete lack of knowledge" (p. 39) among the
faculty about the specific social context of the surrounding
community. They then decided to integrate community
members into their ongoing discussions about how to do a
better job of making their preparation programs more relevant
to the local context which they defined as the neighborhoods
around the university and Boston as a whole.

The teacher education director approached the director of
a local nonprofit community-based advocacy organization
that was focused on issues of community revitalization in
the social, economic, and environmental spheres. The teacher
education director and the community organization director
then obtained a grant together to support the participation
of community members in ongoing discussions that would
help educate the faculty about the local community and to
generate recommendations for revising the teacher education
curriculum to take advantage of the expertise that exists in
the surrounding community. A number of specific suggestions

emerged from these discussions including a greater focus in the program on having teacher candidates learn to design lessons "that used the neighborhood as a source and focus of content for student learning" (p. 42).

Finally, it is also the case that the widespread growth of service learning initiatives in higher education institutions in the United States and internationally has encouraged and supported service learning/community engagement work within teacher education programs. At the University of Wisconsin, where I spent thirty-four years as a teacher educator, I was part of a campus-wide group of faculty in different disciplines who were involved in community engagement and service learning work in their courses and programs. This group met regularly, and through the sharing of work among the faculty and staff in the group it contributed much to the education of the university educators about community engagement and service learning. This same kind of campus encouragement and support for faculty to integrate service learning into their courses exists on many campuses in the United States.

Service learning experiences are probably the most common type of community experience that has existed in teacher education programs internationally, and in some countries, particularly in the global south, service learning experiences may be the major way in which teacher education programs are connected to the communities in which their students learn to teach (Boyle-Baise & McIntyre, 2008; Pederson & Gravatt, 2020).

It has become common in the literature for discussions of service learning experiences in teacher education programs to draw a distinction between "traditional" experiences in which the primary focus is on trying to help those being served and "critical" or "critical multicultural" experiences where there is a focus on the importance of reciprocity in service learning experiences (de'Arlach, Sanchez, & Feuer, 2009). In critical service learning experiences, everyone is a teacher and learner and there is a focus both on the learning of teacher candidates and on responding to community-defined needs (Carter-Andrews, 2009; Boyle-Baise & Sleeter, 2000; Mitchell, 2008).

One important component of critical service learning is for teacher candidates to confront and reexamine their beliefs and practices with regard to race, class, language inequities, and social justice more pointedly than would be the case from just reading articles and discussions within teacher education classroom (Carter-Andrews, 2009; Sleeter, 2001; Zeichner & Melnick, 1996a). When service learning experiences in teacher education have been framed in this way teacher educators have sometimes reported that teacher candidates reexamine their core beliefs about themselves and others and become more capable of forming authentic relationships with family and community members: for example,

> By scaffolding engagement with families as a learning opportunity instead of a service opportunity, preservice teachers developed more authentic relationships and, when preservice teachers were forced to listen rather than talk to parents, they uncovered their own hidden assumptions, biases, and unconscious expectations about families. (Evans, 2013, p. 129)

Other than the examples that have been discussed here and those discussed in the last chapter of teacher education programs that are based in and controlled by communities such as Indigenous teacher education programs and some GYO programs where many of the teacher educators are a part of the communities for which teachers are being prepared, there is very little evidence in the literature on teacher education and communities that programs based in higher education institutions (which are the majority of programs internationally) have made efforts, like the examples noted earlier, to educate teacher education faculty about the communities in which their teacher candidates learn to teach. The literature mostly consists of examples of individual or a few faculty members in institutions of higher education initiating small collaborations with community partners with the support of funds from internal sources or from external grants. These efforts are usually dependent on the few individuals who initiate them, and they often disappear when these individuals are no longer working in the programs and/or when the special funding for the work is no longer available (Koerner & Abdul-Tawaab, 2006).

Most often, beyond the general support and encouragement in some universities provided to faculty in the United States and internationally to employ a service learning component in their courses, there have been few incentives and support for teacher education faculty from within their institutions to become engaged with local community members in preparing teachers. In the United States, severe cuts in state funding for public universities in recent decades (where most US teachers are prepared) have resulted in a decrease of full-time teacher education faculty and an increase of part-time adjunct faculty who are paid to teach particular courses or to supervise the clinical work of teacher candidates (Besas, 2021). The structure of these part-time positions often does not provide for compensating faculty for the extensive work that is necessary to develop and sustain relationships with community partners and together build community components in teacher preparation programs. The loss of funding in public universities which continue to prepare the majority of US teachers, and the increased commodification of universities internationally has also led to increased teaching loads and class sizes and general intensification of the job of teacher education faculty (Ellis & McNicholl, 2015; Moon, 2016).

Additionally, the reward systems in institutions of higher education place value on research production, raising money through external grants, and teaching, and do not often recognize, encourage, or reward teacher education faculty for becoming involved in the extensive labor that is involved in building and maintaining trusting and mutually beneficial relationships with community partners and co-developing and implementing community-engaged activities for teacher candidates in teacher preparation programs. Many of the examples of community–teacher education partnerships that I have read about in the literature were beneficiaries of temporary external support, and when this support ended, so did many of these partnerships. Also, frequently there are often short timelines on external grants that cause a short-circuiting of the process of building trust and mutually beneficial relationships between communities and teacher educators.

Although there have been exceptions to these generalizations like the ones noted in Chapters 2 and 3, for the most part, the participation of families and communities from nondominant communities in the preparation of teachers when present has been limited to service on advisory boards and committees, and participation as guest speakers in courses and other program activities where the influence of community partners is minimal and ongoing mutually beneficial collaborative relationships between teacher educators and community members are largely absent (Murrell, 2001; Souto-Manning & Martell, 2019). Working with members of nondominant communities in preparing teachers for their communities has not become the norm in teacher preparation programs anywhere in the world except in the relatively few community-based and Indigenous programs that exist on the margins of the field.

Design Characteristics

When we consider the conceptualization, design, and implementation of community components in teacher preparation programs, there are certain conditions based on existing research which often include the reports of teacher educators, and less commonly the reports of community participants, that appear to make it more likely that an environment will be created where community expertise will inform the design and implementation of experiences for teacher candidates with nondominant families and communities in teacher preparation programs.

I will briefly discuss here three areas where it appears that achieving certain conditions increases the probability that teachers will be prepared who are willing and able to teach in culturally responsive and sustaining ways. These areas are concerned with the *relationships* that exist between teacher educators and community members and between teacher educators and teacher candidates and community members, and the issue of *power* and knowledge ("Whose knowledge counts?") in these relationships, and in the design and implementation of *community experiences for prospective teachers*. There are other aspects to community participation in teacher preparation where research has been summarized by scholars that suggest successful practices for supporting greater equity for teaching in nondominant communities such as with regard to service learning, and GYO programs, that are outside of the scope of this book (e.g., Anderson & Hill 2001; See Gist, Bianco, & Linn, 2019; Villegas & Clewell, 1999).

Power, Trust, and Reciprocity in Relationships

As stated in the previous chapter, the main sources of variation in the ways in which communities have been connected to the preparation of teachers are not in the types of activities in which teacher candidates have participated (e.g., service learning, community study, or living with families) or in the types of activities that family and community members have participated in with teacher candidates and teacher educators (e.g., serving on advisory boards, guest speaker, or the instructor in a class). The main sources of variation that distinguish individual community connections in teacher preparation programs from one another are in the nature and quality of relationships that are developed between family and community members and teacher candidates and teacher educators, and in the ways that experiences for teacher candidates are structured and implemented to enable realization of the potential benefits of community expertise and cultural wealth for the development of CRS teachers (Zygmunt, Cipollone, Tancock, Clark and Mucherah 2018).

One of the major themes in the literature for creating community participation in teacher preparation programs that supports the development of CRS teaching in nondominant communities is the development of approximations of co-equal or reciprocal relationships characterized by mutual trust & benefit between teacher educators and community participants (e.g., Coff & Lampert, 2019; Zeichner, Bowman, Guillen, & Napolitan, 2016). Given the history of the exploitation of nondominant communities by colleges and universities with university faculty using them as sites for research and clinical experiences in professional preparation programs with often few benefits in return for the communities (e.g., Tuck, 2009), there is understandably often a great deal of mistrust by community members of the motives of teacher educators when they are approached with invitations to collaborate.

Because of this history of promises that were often left unfulfilled in the actions and deeds of university educators whose careers have benefited from the publications they produced from their work in schools and nondominant communities, it is important for teacher educators to approach the goal of attempting to engage families and communities in teacher education programs with a great deal of humility (Chang, 2015; Zygmunt, Cipollone, Clark, & Tancock, 2018). It is also important for teacher educators to convey a transparent and genuine willingness to listen to and learn from what community members have to say to them about their experiences with schools and educators, and sometimes about the universities in which teacher educators work. It is the job of teacher educators to earn the trust of community members and to go into these relationships with the belief that community members possess important and vital knowledge that they can learn from and that can inform program improvement (Hyland & Meacham, 2004).

Engaged faculty see diverse communities as vital to the development of a knowledge base for educating teachers for diversity and seek to overcome what Koerner & Abdul-Tawwab refer to as a deep seated "fortress culture" of the institutions of higher learning. (Mule, 2010, p. 16)

Traditionally, relationships between university teacher educators and members of nondominant communities, when they have existed at all, have been hierarchical with university faculty inviting family and community members to participate in activities that have often already been conceptualized and designed by the teacher educators based on their own assessments of what needs to be done and how. I have witnessed and been a participant in many meetings of teacher educators and community members during my career where community "guests" spend most of the time listening to the presentations of information by teacher educators with a little time provided after the presentations for community members to react. This university-centric and extractive approach to collaboration with communities that mostly focuses on the needs of the teacher educators, and not those of the community, often alienates community members and leaves much of the expertise that they have to offer programs untapped (e.g., Guillen & Zeichner, 2018; Lees, 2016).

In order to disrupt this dominant knowledge-power hierarchy in community partnerships in teacher education, teacher educators must help create a situation where community voice and expertise is seen as important as school and university teacher educator expertise, and where community participants play an active role in shaping the conversations in which they are asked to participate with teacher educators and the interactions that they have with teacher candidates (Mahan, 1993).

In order to achieve the kind of reciprocal relationships that are needed to benefit from the expertise of community members, teacher educators must "yield some of their intellectual territory" and power they are used to employing (Hyland & Meacham, 2004). Community participants should be engaged from the very beginning in a codesign process (Ishimaru et al., 2019) identifying the problems, deciding which ones should be prioritized for action, and in conceptualizing, designing, and implementing activities to address them. This community-centric approach to collaborating with families and communities in teacher preparation programs that provides a "rightful presence" (Calabrese-Barton & Tan, 2020) for community members in programs is in sharp contrast to the more common guest-host relationships where community members are invited to provide input within the parameters set by teacher educators.

In order for community participants to achieve an equal and respected status with teacher educators in co-conceptualizing and co-designing program elements, teacher educators will need to broaden their acceptance of the forms of knowledge and ways of teaching to include those that are commonly used in community settings that are beyond those which are typically deemed to be acceptable in the academy. Teacher educators need to give up some of the power that they are typically used to exerting in order to help create a climate that values genuine community participation.[1] Also as part of the effort to disrupt traditional power hierarchies in teacher education and community relationships, it is important that community participants be fairly compensated for the work that they do to help to educate teacher educators and teacher candidates about their communities and in co-designing and implementing new program components.

There are examples of this kind of community-centric approach in education and community partnerships outside of teacher education. One current example of what is needed in teacher education can be found in the United States in the work of the Family Leadership Design Collaborative where members of nondominant communities and university educators codesign action-oriented research to address community-defined needs and aspirations (Ishimaru et al., 2019).[2] Other examples can be found in teacher education programs that have a successful track record of community-centric collaboration with one or a few communities for the benefit of a relatively small number of teacher candidates such as the programs at the Ball State University and the Chicago Teacher Education (Mustian, O'Mally, Garcia, Millan, & Zamudio-Mainou, 2021; Zygmunt & Clark, 2015).

The issue of broadening the forms of knowledge and pedagogy beyond those that are dominant in the academy is a critical issue in accessing the expertise and community cultural wealth that community partners bring with them to teacher education program collaborations. In the research my colleagues and I have done on teacher educators in our own programs, collaborating with members of nondominant communities in preparing teachers, we discovered it often was the passion, authenticity, and style of interaction between community mentors and our teacher candidates that was a critical factor in creating an environment where teacher candidates were motivated to reexamine their views about themselves, and their perceptions of families in nondominant communities (e.g., Zeichner, Bowman, Guillen, & Napolitan, 2016). For example, storytelling was frequently an influential pedagogy used by some of the community mentors my colleagues and I have worked with in disrupting the deficit perspectives about nondominant communities that many teacher candidates brought with them to their preparation programs. Community-based teacher educators must be given the freedom to mentor and teach in the ways that are comfortable to them and not be pressured by academics to fit into normative ways of teaching within the academy.

In the work that we have done collaborating with communities in teacher education, there has been some criticism at times from some of my colleagues about the storytelling pedagogy that some of our community partners regularly used in teaching and mentoring teacher candidates. I have always argued back to them that we should not expect or attempt to pressure our community partners to teach in the ways in which we teach because the whole point of inviting them to partner with us in educating teachers is that they bring things to the program that we often lack and that we need to be able to prepare teachers to teach in their communities. There is evidence in some of our research that it was the passion and authenticity in the stories of community mentors that helped teacher candidates genuinely reexamine their views about themselves and others in ways that support the development of CRS teaching. For example, here are two brief comments from our research interviews with teacher candidates in one of the University of Washington programs about their interactions with community mentors:

> Besides for the words that they're saying, there's the emotion in the room. There's more meaning conveyed there than anything that you can read on paper or hear about from someone telling you they heard it. (Zeichner, Bowman, Guillen, & Napolitan, 2016, p. 286)

> I think unfortunately I always had the feeling that they really didn't care about their kids, that they weren't there and maybe they wouldn't come in because they didn't care about their kids, really care. I think there's been a big shift in my thinking, just hearing stories from people who are in these positions. (Zeichner, Bowman, Guillen, & Napolitan, 2016, p. 286)

Thus, an important element of variation in community partnerships in teacher education is the degree to which teacher educators try to impose their ways of acting in the academy on community mentors or, on the other hand, encourage their community partners to collaborate in the ways that they find most meaningful. The optimal situation is one where leadership is shared and where both teacher educators and community participants feel ownership of the work, feel free to work in ways in which they are comfortable, and feel accountable to one another for doing a good job.

Also, it is always important to remember that the conditions of mutual trust and respect and shared leadership are not ends, that once established, are embedded in a program forever. The work of establishing and maintaining genuinely democratic spaces where decisions about the work of educating teachers are negotiated and collaboratively enacted is complex, messy, difficult, and never-ending.[3] If there are no bumps in the road and things always seem to be going smoothly without any conflicts or disagreements, then this may be a sign that there are important feelings not being communicated.

Teacher Candidate Experiences in Communities

There are several things that stand out in the literature that appear to be important in creating the kind of community experiences for teacher candidates that contribute toward their development as CRS teachers. These elements indicate some of the most important points of variation in community experiences. It should be noted that some community experiences take place in a community or school setting while others take place in schools or in a college or university space when community participants do their teaching and mentoring.

One of the most important aspects of community experiences is the nature of their links to the rest of the teacher education program. Ideally, community experiences would be linked to the entire program, and all teacher educators in the program would be committed to their importance and value (Murrell, 2001) of accessing community expertise in the preparation of teachers. As mentioned previously, this program-wide connection to community experiences appears to be uncommon. The most common pattern is for one or a few teacher educators to form links with community members, and then to plan and carry out a community collaboration in ways that are linked to their courses. The details of these community collaborations are often invisible to the rest of their colleagues.

Haddix (2015) has argued that a connection to coursework is important for these experiences to be able to contribute to the necessary work to be done by candidates of critical thinking, questioning, and dialoging about what was learned from their experiences in communities and the implications of this learning for their teaching practice. The most common model of community experiences in programs has been a link to a single course. Sometimes the experience is carefully structured and carefully coordinated with course content, but other times it is not, and candidates are sent into community organizations without much guidance or support for either the candidates or the community partners.

Another one of the most important aspects of these experiences is how they are planned and monitored, and by whom. Ideally, the experiences are co-conceptualized and co-planned from the beginning by teacher educators and their community partners in ways that benefit both the program and the community. It is also important that both teacher candidates and community participants are prepared for the experiences and are then supported as they proceed through the experience. One common form of support is to hold debriefing sessions after a session to help teacher candidates and/or community members process what they experienced intellectually and emotionally. Guillen and Zeichner (2018) reflected on the importance of support for community mentors in the University of Washington programs:

> Spaces for community mentors to reflect, support, and encourage one another as teacher educators became an important part of the partnership. Mentors took risks in sharing, explaining, and putting aside their own feelings to attend to those of preservice teachers. These experiences left some mentors feeling exhausted and questioning whether or not to continue. On those occasions, fellow community mentors provided spaces for reflection and support for one another immediately following the event. (p. 151)

In this program and in the work done in other programs (e.g., Lees, 2016), it can be seen that it is just as important to prepare and support community participants as it is to prepare and support teacher candidates. Because teacher candidates sometimes come to their community experiences with negative and deficit-oriented views of nondominant communities, that are sometimes reinforced by elements in their program, community participants in teacher education programs sometimes experience emotional distress and anger and even feel a need to "detox" sometimes when they encounter the negative attitudes of some teacher candidates, and they need support. At the University of Washington, we did not anticipate the need for this support initially, but once we began to see the ongoing need for this mentor support we added it as a regular feature of the collaboration (Guillen, 2016).

Opportunities for debriefing with and providing support for teacher candidates are also critical in understanding how they experienced their work in communities and with community participants outside of community settings. Teacher candidates are often very emotional after their sometimes intense interactions in community settings and with community members in their classes, and they often need support in processing what they experienced and in connecting what they learned to their teaching.

Another aspect of community experiences that appears to be important is that they should take place over time and enable teacher candidates and community mentors to develop trusting relationships with each other. Lees (2016), in her research on the perspectives of community mentors in a teacher education-community partnership situated in Indigenous communities, has argued that brief encounters between teacher candidates and community mentors provide "brief encounters for candidates to experience otherness through soft reform efforts that run the risk of tokenizing the knowledge and experience of Indigenous peoples" (p. 375). The development of trusting relationships between teacher candidates and community mentors over time has often been found to be a key factor in helping candidates take down their guard and ask their mentors for advice about difficult issues often connected to race and privilege (e.g., Seidl & Friend, 2002).

Another critical issue affecting the quality of community experiences is the nature and quality of the mediation of community experiences provided by teacher educators and community participants. Unless these experiences are carefully framed and then mediated for candidates during and after they occur, there is a danger that they can serve to strengthen and reinforce the prejudices and stereotypes that candidates bring to their programs.

Building and Sustaining Community-Teacher Education Partnerships

As has been stated repeatedly in this book, teacher education-community partnerships, with few exceptions, have not become the norm in preparing teachers anywhere in the world despite the growing recognition internationally of the importance of preparing teachers to work collaboratively with families and communities, particularly in nondominant communities. From the beginning, relatively few people in relatively few programs have partnered with members of nondominant communities, and with a few exceptions, these partnerships have usually lasted for brief periods of time. In the programs that have formed partnerships with members of nondominant communities, it is often not clear from reading about their work how these partnerships have dealt with the many dimensions of variation that have been discussed in this book.

System Supports for Community Partnerships in Teacher Education

There are a number of issues that need to be addressed in teacher education programs, in the institutions in which they exist, and in the policy environments that impact what happens in teacher preparation programs for partnerships that include nondominant communities in preparing teachers to become the norm in teacher preparation. First, there is a need for the institutions in which teacher education programs exist to provide encouragement and support for programs to establish and sustain partnerships with nondominant communities in which their teacher candidates complete their school and community-based clinical experiences. For example, campus offices that are responsible for overseeing campus partnerships with community agencies can provide the logistical support that is needed to establish sustained partnerships with community groups (Mule, 2010).

States and other local government agencies also potentially can play an important role in incentivizing the development of genuinely collaborative and mutually beneficial teacher education-school-community partnerships through grants that support the development of new partnerships and their ongoing evaluation in ways that are responsive to nondominant communities.

For community partnerships in teacher education to become more widespread, incentives and support from beyond the programs will need to become more available on a wider scale. In the United States, philanthropic foundations such as the W. K. Kellogg Foundation and federal government grants like the US Department of Education Teacher Quality Partnership Grants have been important sources for teacher education partnerships that are focused in nondominant communities. Both of these sources have funded teacher residency programs (Guha, Hyler, & Darling-Hammond, 2016), a hybrid form of teacher preparation program that ideally is jointly owned and run by teacher educators (university-based or non-university-based in a nonprofit), school districts, and sometimes also community partners and local teacher unions. Although some residency programs include community participation at the governing level in developing, managing, and/or implementing the program, community participation beyond serving on an advisory board exists in relatively few teacher residency programs. It has not been common for community participation to be required in the development of funding proposals for support for teacher residency programs. Nor has it been common for funding to be provided for community participants to be actively engaged in the design of programs or in the preparation process as instructors and mentors for teacher candidates.[4]

Given the tremendous variability that has existed in how teacher educators have designed and implemented community partnerships, it is important for government and private funders to require that recipients include local communities (particularly nondominant communities) in these partnerships. It is also important that funders require that recipients include certain elements in their programs that will support the establishment of the kinds of specific program features like those that have been discussed in this chapter. For example, funders should require community partners from nondominant communities to be engaged in the proposal development process and to be included in the governance and ongoing implementation of programs including co-responsibility for making decisions about the dispersal of grant funds.

In addition to providing incentives and support for small pilot programs that enable teacher educators and their community partners to test out ideas with a small group of teacher candidates, there should be more attention to trying to help some of the successful pilot efforts to grow over time to include more teacher candidates and teacher educators in the teacher education institutions included in the grants. There also must be more attention to requiring grantees to provide institutional support for assuming more of the costs of the program over time to contribute to the sustainability of the work.

Government and private funders of community engagement work in teacher education should also consider funding groups of programs and creating networks of programs that can support and sustain each other's work. There is some evidence in the United States that forming networks of teacher preparation programs that are committed to the same principles of reform (e.g., Goodlad, 1994; The Holmes Group, 2007; Teachers for a New Era, 2018) can strengthen the capacity of individual programs in creating program reforms. The problem has come in sustaining the reforms created once the funds are gone, and in scaling up the reforms beyond the small number of programs that are included in the funded projects.

There is an extensive literature internationally on teacher education partnerships (e.g., Lynch & Smith, 2012; Smith, 2016). Because much of this literature ignores the role of communities in these partnerships, particularly the role of nondominant communities, I have focused in this book only on the community and teacher educator components in teacher education partnerships. Obviously, all teacher education partnerships also include school partners such as school districts, and in some cases they also include local teacher associations or unions. Bringing the school partners into view in teacher education partnerships further complicates the dynamics of relationships and power in these partnerships.

Both university and school teacher educators in these partnerships need to ensure that the conditions discussed in this chapter for providing more genuinely democratic spaces for program development and ongoing implementation and improvement to occur are present and that community partners are not treated as second-class citizens as is often the case. The history of teacher education partnerships shows that rather than disrupting the typical hierarchical relations between university, school, and community partners, the domination of university partners over school and community partners has often been strengthened and supported.

> Despite the upsurge of the community engagement movement in institutions of higher learning since the 1990s, while college-community partnerships have increased, they have also tended to reinforce and sustain the traditional hegemony of academe and the marginalization of economically depressed communities. (Mule, 2010, p. 75)

Some teacher educators like Gorodetsy and Barak (2008) in Israel have argued the position that it will never be possible to create the kind of environments in existing school or university, or non-profit-based programs to create the kinds of conditions discussed in this chapter. They argue for the establishment of new hybrid or third spaces for teacher education partnerships involving schools and universities in which genuinely collaborative cultures can be created (also see Zeichner, Payne, & Brayko, 2015).

> There is a growing recognition that these partnerships were inefficient in establishing new collaborative cultures, and in many cases they even pursued the old hegemonies of the individual institutions. It seems that bringing together the two institutions or cultures was not sufficient to establish shared cultural norms . . . Despite the declared common objectives, each institution continued to maintain its own culture and unique discourse. The teacher education programs continued to hold their hegemony for the construction of knowledge and its dissemination, while keeping the schools in the position of merely serving as "practice fields" for prospective teachers. (p. 1907)

Whether or not programs exist in new forms of hybrid spaces like the ones created in some of the newer teacher residency programs or continue to exist as school-based or in university and school-based programs, school and university teacher educators in these programs need to provide safe and welcoming spaces for community-based teacher educators to share the valuable perspectives and knowledge they bring to teacher preparation that teacher candidates and their teacher educators need to be able to access and learn from to educate teachers to teach successfully for their communities. These protected institutional spaces must also be ones that encourage and reward school and university-based teacher educators for spending the time needed to build and maintain trusting and reciprocal relationships with members of nondominant communities as co-teacher educators. Lees (2016) refers to these necessary changes as a paradigm shift for teacher education, particularly those based in universities.

In addition to the provision of funding and support for the development of new community partnerships in teacher education, the government agencies and independent bodies that conduct the evaluation and accreditation of teacher preparation programs should provide additional incentives for programs to engage local nondominant communities in collaborating in preparing teachers by incorporating into their approval standards more elaborated and specific requirements for the preparation of teachers to work with families and communities and require the participation of members of nondominant communities in the ongoing development and implementation of teacher preparation programs as was the case in the Teacher Corps program in the United States that was discussed in Chapter 2.

Government and professional evaluators of teacher preparation programs also need to ensure that members of nondominant communities have a role in the program evaluation and accreditation process such as being part of the teams that visit the program locations and/or being interviewed as part of the process about their perceptions of the quality of the teachers that a particular program has prepared. This accountability of programs to nondominant communities should become a part of the program evaluation process.

Conclusion

In this book, I've attempted to illuminate and discuss some of the important ways in which teacher preparation partnerships with nondominant communities in teacher education have varied, and to articulate some of the dimensions in these partnerships that seem most likely at present to enable access by both teacher educators and teacher candidates to the expertise and cultural wealth in nondominant communities so that the teaching that new teachers learn to provide in schools in nondominant communities better reflects the expertise and cultural wealth in these communities and students in these communities see their lives outside of school reflected in their education in school.

In doing so, I've stressed the importance of building mutual benefit, trust, and respect in the relationships between teacher educators and community participants, and the participation of community members from the very beginning in conceptualizing and planning the work in a process of codesign. I've also argued for more incentives and support for community participation in teacher education by institutions, and the philanthropic and government agencies that regulate and fund teacher preparation programs.

The field has progressed since the days when Peter Murrell criticized the Holmes Group in the United States for ignoring the role of communities in professional development school partnerships (Murrell, 1998). The inclusion of community experiences and community participation in teacher education has become somewhat more common in programs in the United States, but much of this participation has been superficial and has not necessarily lifted up and helped teacher educators and candidates benefit from the untapped expertise that exists in nondominant communities. Too few teacher candidates currently receive preparation for teaching that reflects genuine and ongoing collaboration among teacher educators, teachers, and community members.

Underlying my arguments in this book about community participation in teacher education programs is a vision of a new hybrid structure for teacher preparation programs that includes program staff, community members, and educators from the schools in which teacher candidates learn to teach sharing ownership and responsibility for the work of preparing teachers. My colleagues and I have elaborated the nature of these hybrid programs elsewhere (e.g., Kretchmar & Zeichner, 2016; Payne & Zeichner, 2017; and Zeichner, Payne, & Brayko, 2015). Whether or not it will be possible to create and sustain new collaborative structures within the internationally dominant form of university teacher education or to create the paradigm shift that will be needed in more traditional forms of teacher education remains to be seen.

NOTES

Preface

1 Schools in which at least 40 percent of children from low-income families as measured by student enrollment in the federal free and reduced lunch and breakfast programs are eligible to receive federal Title 1 funding.
2 I was supposed to share a classroom with another intern in the program, but because the school needed another teacher and could not find one to hire, my partner and I were each given our own classroom as teachers of record and were mentored by the colleagues on our teaching team rather than by individual mentor teachers.
3 Also see Grace (2006) for a discussion of the comparison with community voice and influence in middle-class communities.

Chapter One

1 Black, Indigenous, and people of color (it is commonly used to refer to members of non-White communities in North America).
2 https://www.edweek.org/leadership/education-statistics-facts
-about-american-schools/2019/01.
3 https://www.nbcnews.com/news/nbcblk/map-see-which-states
-have-passed-critical-race-theory-bills-n1271215.
4 https://www.nytimes.com/2022/04/12/us/politics/transgender
-laws-us.html.
5 https://www.thedailybeast.com/grapevine-colleyville-texas-school
-board-ousts-black-principal-james-whitfield-over-critical-race-theory.

6 https://www.bridgemi.com/talent-education/michigan-gop-bill
-schools-must-post-curriculum-books-assignments.

7 Cited by Hong (2019), p. 69.

8 See Baquedano-Lopez et.al. (2013) for a discussion of the
research on how race, class, and immigration status impact
parent and family connections to schools.

9 Hong (2019) provides five detailed examples of teachers in
Boston and Washington DC who work in genuinely collaborate
ways with their students' parents and caregivers.

Chapter Two

1 In Canada and Australia, another name that is sometimes used
to describe Indigenous teacher education programs is Remote
Area Teacher Education Programs (e.g., https://tafeqld.edu.au
/information-for/aboriginal-and-torres-strait-islander-people/
ratep). In some cases, Indigenous teacher education programs
have been referred to as Grow Your Own Programs (e.g., Giles,
Prescott, and Rhodes, 2011).

2 The Peace Corps was authorized by the US government in 1961
as an independent agency and volunteer program providing
international social and economic development assistance around
the world.

3 Sarason (1995) refers to this right of people affected by an
organization having the right to participate in its governance as
the "political principal."

4 https://nafsce.org/page/preserviceconsortium.

5 https://nafsce.org/page/MiniGrant?utm_source=Informz&utm_
medium=Email&utm_campaign=Email&_zs=E83Uc&_zl=J9pG3.

6 https://nafsce.org/page/IHEsurvey.

Chapter Three

1 Teachers from nondominant communities should and do teach
in schools in all kinds of communities, but the focus here is
only on the issue of preparing teachers to teach in nondominant
communities.

2 https://www.nea.org/advocating-for-change/new-from-nea/school
   -prison-pipeline-time-shut-it-down.

3 https://www.kuow.org/stories/the-other-end-of-the-pipeline
   -teachers-go-to-prison-to-get-schooled.

4 The agency of community members in this program includes
   participation in writing the chapter referred to here and in
   making conference presentations about the program as well as
   in presentations to university classes about teacher education.
   I also observed the agentic role of community members in my
   conversations with community members during my visits to the
   program and conversations with participants.

5 https://www.washingtonpost.com/news/answer-sheet/wp/2015
   /09/25/the-surprising-things-seattle-teachers-won-for-students-by
   -striking/.

6 https://seis.ucla.edu/news/la-center-x-teaching-leading-and-living.

7 https://www.k12.wa.us/student-success/resources-subject-area/
   time-immemorial-tribal-sovereignty-washington-state.

8 https://education.uw.edu/programs/necp/?utm_source=pce.uw
   .edu&utm_medium=referral&utm_campaign=(not%20set.

9 https://www.nea.org/student-success/great-public-schools/
   community-schools/what-are-they.

10 More information on public community schools and the various
   ways in which communities interact with educators within these
   schools see (Community Schools Forward, 2023; Oakes, Maier,
   & Daniel, 2017; and Maier, Daniel, Oakes, & Lam, 2017).

11 See https://rethinkingschools.org/issues/volume-2-no-3/.

12 Half of the students were native English speakers and the other
   half were native Spanish speakers.

13 https://rethinkingschools.org/about-rethinking-schools/our
   -history/.

14 A Swahili verb meaning to pull together.

15 An African American and Pan African long holiday celebrated
   mainly in the United States, Canada, and the Caribbean as a
   celebration of African American family social and cultural traditions.

16 Communication with program co-directors Andreal and
   Arlington Davis, August 2022.

17 Communication with Andreal and Arlington Davis, August
   2022.

18 Communication with Andreal and Arlington Davis, August
   2022.

19 Currently, there are over 800 GYO programs in the United States. It is difficult to determine the exact number because states have somewhat different definitions of what counts as a GYO program (Personal communication with Amaya Gomez, October 2022).
20 See Waite, S., Mentor, M., & Bristol, T. J. (2018).
21 https://cehs.unl.edu/roots/about-program/.

Chapter Four

1 In the context of university-based preparation programs, this often requires teacher educators ,who often have less seniority and power in education schools and departments, to openly challenge the "fortress culture" of universities that supports and rewards expert-recipient relationships with both schools and external communities, This work can be risky for teacher educators, but it is necessary to provide the ground on which to build mutually beneficial and respectful relationships across universities and communities (Lees, 2016; Mule, 2010)
2 This work is similar to the tradition of participatory action research which was initiated in the global south and has been used worldwide (e.g., Galletta and Torre, 2019).
3 Edward's (2010) work in developing the concept of "relational agency" is very helpful here in understanding the shifts that are needed by teacher educators as professionals have come to increasingly work across institutional boundaries in new hybrid spaces.
4 A group of the major organizations in the United States involved in supporting the development of teacher residency programs (The Pathways Alliance) recently published a definition of residency programs. It is clear in this definition that leadership in the design and implementation of residency programs does not include local community participants. Although community members and CBOs are included among possible stakeholders who sometimes participate in programs, they are clearly placed in a secondary role along with other groups if they participate at all. https://drive.google.com/file/d/1Tvzvp9oKozwn3D -fo9AHafDrQ4aSnGm7/view.

REFERENCES

Alanko, A. (2018). Preparing pre-service teachers for home-school cooperation: Exploring Finnish teacher education programmes. *Journal of Education for Teaching, 44*(3), 321–332.

Alim, H. S., & Paris, D. (Eds.). (2017). What is culturally sustaining pedagogy and why does it matter? In D. Paris & H. S. Alim (Eds.), *Culturally sustaining pedagogies: Teaching and learning in a changing world* (pp. 1–24). New York: Teachers College Press.

American Association of Colleges for Teacher Education. (2018). *A pivot toward clinical practice, its lexicon, and renewing the profession of teaching.* Washington, DC: Author.

Anderson, J. B., & Hill, D. (2001). *Principles of good practices for service-learning in preservice teacher education.* Service Learning, General Paper 35. Retrieved from http://digitalcommons .unomaha.edu/slceslgen/35.

Anyon, J. (2014). *Radical possibilities: Public policy, urban education, and a new social movement.* New York: Routledge.

Appe, S., Rubaii, N., Lippez-De Castro, S., & Capobianco, S. (2017). The concept and the context of the engaged university in the Global South: Lessons from Latin America to guide a research agenda. *Journal of Higher Education Outreach and Engagement, 21*(2), 7–36.

Archibald, J. (2008). Native teacher education program (NITEP). In S. Niessen (Ed.), *Self-study compilation and report, aboriginal ways of knowing in teacher education* (pp. 88–95). Regina: Canadian Council on Learning.

Archibald, J. (2015, April). Indigenous teacher education: Struggle and triumph for justice and more. A paper presented at the annual meeting of the American Educational Research Association, Chicago.

Au, K., & Kawakami, A. (1994). Cultural congruence in instruction. In E. Hollins, J. King, & W. Hayman (Eds.), *Teaching diverse populations: Formulating the knowledge base* (pp. 5–23). Albany, NY: SUNY Press.

Bagley, S. S., & Rust, V. D. (2009). The Scandinavian folk high school: Community-based education in Norway, Sweden, and Denmark. In R. Raby & E. Valeau (Eds.), *Community college models: Globalization and higher education* (pp. 279–298). New York: Springer.

Baker, B. (2018). *Educational inequality and school finance: Why money matters for America's students.* Cambridge, MA: Harvard Education Press.

Banks, C. A., & Banks, J. A. (1995). Equity pedagogy: An essential component of multicultural education. *Theory into Practice, 34*(3), 152–158.

Baptiste, H. P., Baptiste, M., & Gollnick, D. (1980). *Multicultural teacher education: Preparing teachers to provide educational equity* (Vol. 1). Washington, DC: American Association of Colleges for Teacher Education.

Baquedano-Lopez, P., Alexander, R. A., & Hernandez, S. J. (2013). Equity issues in parental and community involvement in schools: What teacher educators need to know. *Review of Research in Education, 37*(1), 149–182.

Barajas-Lopez, F., & Ishimaru, A. M. (2020). Darles el lugar: A place for nondominant family knowing in educational equity. *Urban Education, 55*(1), 38–65.

Barnes, M. E. (2017). Encouraging interaction and striving for reciprocity: The challenges of community-engaged projects in teacher education. *Teaching and Teacher Education, 68*, 220–231.

Barnes, M. E. (2020). Contested pasts, complicated presents: Pre-service teachers developing conceptions of community. *Teaching and Teacher Education, 96*, 1–11.

Besas, M. (2021, March 15). Tenured faculty keep being replaced by adjuncts across the U.S. *The College Post.* Retrieved from https://thecollegepost.com/tenured-faculty-replaced-adjuncts/.

Blair, L., & Erickson, O. (1964). *The student teacher's experience in the community.* Reston, VA: Association of Teacher Educators.

Bortolin, K. (2011, Fall). Serving ourselves: How the discourse on community engagement privileges the university over community. *Michigan Journal of Community Service Learning, 18*(1), 49–58.

Boyle-Baise, M. (2005). Preparing community-oriented teachers: Reflections from a multicultural service-learning project. *Journal of Teacher Education, 56*(5), 446–458.

Boyle-Baise, M., & McIntyre, D. J. (2008). What kind of experience? Preparing teachers in PDS or community settings. In M. Cochran-Smith, S. Feiman-Nemser, & D. J. McIntyre (Eds.), *Handbook of research on teacher education* (3rd ed., pp. 307–330). New York: Routledge.

Boyle-Baise, M., & Sleeter, C. (2000). Community-based service learning for multicultural education. *Educational Foundations, 14*(2), 33–50.

Brayko, K. (2013). Community-based placements as contexts for disciplinary learning: A study of literacy teacher education outside of school. *Journal of Teacher Education, 61*(1), 47–59.

Brown, K. (2014). Teaching in color: A critical race theory in education analysis of the literature on preservice teachers of color and teacher education in the US. *Race, Ethnicity and Education, 17*(3), 326–345.

Bryk, A., & Schneider, B. (2002). A grounded theory of relational trust. In A. Bryk & B. Schneider (Eds.), *Trust in schools: A core resource for improvement* (pp. 124–144). New York: Russell Sage Foundation.

Calabrese-Barton, A., Drake, C., Perez, J. G., St. Louis, K., & George, M. (2004). Ecologies of parental engagement in urban education. *Educational Researcher, 33*(4), 3–12.

Calabrese-Barton, A., & Tan, E. (2020). Beyond equity as inclusion: A framework of "rightful presence" for guiding justice-oriented studies in teaching and learning. *Educational Researcher, 49*(6), 433–440.

Cardichon, J., Darling-Hammond, L., Yang, M., Shields, P. M., & Burns, D. (2020). *Inequitable opportunity to learn: Student access to certified and experienced teachers.* Palo Alto, CA: Learning Policy Institute.

Carter, P., & Darling-Hammond, L. (2016). Teaching diverse learners. In D. H. Gitomer & C. A. Bell (Eds.), *Handbook of research on teaching* (5th ed., pp. 593–638). Washington, DC: American Educational Research Association.

Carter, P. L., & Welner, K. G. (Eds.). (2013). *Closing the opportunity gap: What America must do to give every child an even chance.* New York: Oxford University Press.

Carter Andrews, D. (2009). "The hardest thing to learn from": The effects of service learning on the preparation of urban educators. *Equity and Excellence in Education*, 42(3), 272–293.

Carver-Thomas, D. (2018, April). *Diversifying the teaching profession: How to recruit and retain teachers of color*. Palo Alto, CA: Learning Policy Institute.

Caspe, M., Monaco, M., & Finklea, T. (2021). *How the revised CAEP standards affirm the importance of educator preparation for family engagement*. National Association for Family, School, and Community Engagement. Retrieved from https://nafsce.org/page/CAEPStandards.

Catapano, S., & Huisman, S. (2010). Preparing teachers for urban schools: Evaluation of a community-based model. *Perspectives on Urban Education*, 7(1). Retrieved from https://urbanedjournal.gse.upenn.edu/archive/volume-7-issue-1-summer-2010/preparing-teachers-urban-schools-evaluation-community-based-mod.

Chang, B. (2015). In the service of self-determination: Teacher education, service learning, and community reorganizing. *Theory into Practice*, 54(1), 29–38.

Clark, P., Zygmunt, E., Tancock, S., & Cipollone, K. (Eds.). (2021). *The power of community-engaged teacher preparation*. New York: Teachers College Press.

Clewell, B. C., & Villegas, A. M. (1999). Creating a nontraditional pipeline for urban teachers: The pathways to teaching careers model. *Journal of Negro Education*, 68(3), 306–317.

Cochran-Smith, M., & Villegas, A. M. (2016). Research on teacher preparation: Charting the landscape of a sprawling field. In D. H. Gitomer & C. A. Bell (Eds.), *Handbook of research on teaching* (5th ed., pp. 439–548). Washington, DC: American Educational Research Association.

Coff, K., & Lampert, J. (2019). Mentoring as two-way learning: An Australian first nations/non-indigenous collaboration. *Frontiers in Education*, 4(24), 1–8.

Collins, P. M. (2010). The new politics of community. *American Sociological Review*, 75(1), 7–30.

Comer, J. P., Haynes, N. M., Joyner, E. T., & Ben-Avie, M. (1996). *Rallying the whole village: The comer process for reforming education*. New York: Teachers College Press.

Community Schools Forward. (2023). Framework: Essentials for community school transformation. https://learningpolicyinstitute.org/project/community-schools-forwa.

Cook, B., & Kothari, U. (Eds.). (2001). *Participation: The new Tyranny?* London: Zed Books.

Cooper, J. (2007). Strengthening the case for community-based learning in teacher education. *Journal of Teacher Education, 58*(3), 245–255.

Council of Chief State School Officers. (2012). *Our preparation our promise: Transforming educator preparation and entry into the profession.* Washington, DC: Author.

Cross, B. E. (2005). New racism, reformed teacher education, and the same ole' oppression. *Educational Studies, 38*(3), 263–274.

Cuban, L. (1969). Teacher and community. *Harvard Educational Review, 39*(2), 253–272.

d'Arlach, L., Sanchez, B., & Feuer, R. (2009, Fall). Voices from the community: A case for reciprocity in service learning. *Michigan Journal of Community Service Learning, 16*(1), 5–16.

Darling-Hammond, L. (2013). Inequality in school resources: What will it take to close the opportunity gap? In P. L. Carter & K. G. Welner (Eds.), *Closing the opportunity gap: What every America must do to give every child an even chance?* (pp. 77–97). New York: Oxford University Press.

De Brunine, E. J., Willemse, T. M., D'Haem, J., Griswold, P., Vloeberghs, L., & van Eynde, S. (2014). Preparing teacher candidates for family-school partnerships. *European Journal of Teacher Education, 37*(4), 409–404.

Delanty, G. (2018). *Community* (3rd ed.). London: Routledge.

Delany-Barmann, G. (2010). Teacher education reform and subaltern voices: From politica to practica in Bolivia. *Journal of Language, Identity, and Education, 9*(3), 180–202.

Delpit, L. (1988). Power and pedagogy in educating other people's children. *Harvard Educational Review, 58*(3), 280–299.

Dobber, M., Vandyck, I. J. J., Akkerman, S. F., de Graaff,, R., Beishuizen, J. J., Pilot, A., & Vermunt, J. D. (2013). The development of community competence in the teacher education curriculum. *European Journal of Teacher Education, 36*(3), 346–363.

Driscoll, M. E. (1998). Professionalism versus community: Themes from recent school catalyst for change in higher education institutions. *Peabody Journal of Education, 73*(1), 89–127.

Dryness, A. (2011). *Mothers united: An immigrant struggle for socially just education.* Minneapolis, MN: University of Minnesota Press.

Edelfelt, R. A., Corwin, R., & Hanna, E. (1974). *Lessons from the teacher corps*. Washington, DC: The National Education Association.

Edwards, A. (2010). *Being an expert professional practitioner: The relational turn in expertise*. London: Springer.

Ellis, V., Maguire, M., Zeichner, K., Are, T., Yang, X., & Qui, R. (2016). Teaching other people's children elsewhere for a while. *Journal of Education Policy, 31*(1), 89–127.

Ellis, V., & McNicholl, J. (2015). *Transforming teacher education: Reconfiguring the academic work*. London: Bloomsbury.

Epstein, J. L., & Sanders, M. G. (2006). Prospects for change: Preparing educators for school, family, and community partnerships. *Peabody Journal of Education, 81*(2), 81–120.

Evans, M. P. (2013). Educating preservice teachers for family, school, and community engagement. *Teaching Education, 24*(2), 123–133.

Ewing, E. (2018). *Ghosts in the schoolyard: Racism and school closings on Chicago's southside*. Chicago, IL: University of Chicago Press.

Featherstone, J. (1968, January 13). Community control of our schools. *The New Republic, 158*(2), 16–19. https://orbiscascade-washington.primo.exlibrisgroup.com/permalink/01ALLIANCE_UW/db578v/cdi_proquest_miscellaneous_1301054257.

Flowers, J. G., Patterson, A., Strateymer, F., & Lindsey, M. (1948). *School and community laboratory experiences in teacher education*. Oneata, NY: American Association of Colleges for Teacher Education.

Francois, A. M., & Hunter Quartz, K. (Eds.). (2021) *Preparing and sustaining social justice educators*. Cambridge, MA: Harvard Education Press.

Gallego, M. A. (2001). Is experience the best teacher? The potential of coupling classroom and community-based field experiences. *Journal of Teacher Education, 52*(4), 312–325.

Galletta, A., & Torre, E. (2019, August). Participatory action research in education. In G. W. Noblit (Ed.), *Oxford research encyclopedia education*. Retrieved from https://doi.org/10.1093/acrefore/9780190264093.013.557.

Gay, G. (2018). *Culturally responsive teaching: Theory, research and practice* (3rd ed.). New York: Teachers College Press.

Giles, W., Prescott, D., & Rhodes, D. (2011). *Innovative teacher training in remote Australian indigenous communities: A sustainable staffing model*. Barcelona: Global University Network for Innovation. Retrieved from http://www.guninetwork.org/articles/innovative-teacher-training-remote-australian-indigenous-communities-sustainable-staffing.

Gillette, M. D. (2011). Doing it better together: The challenges and the promise of community-based teacher education. In E. A. Skinner, M. T. Garreton, & B. D. Schultz (Eds.), *Grow your own teachers: Grassroots change in teacher education* (pp. 146–162). New York: Teachers College Press.

Gillette, M. D. (2018). Walking into the community: Community partnerships as a catalyst for change in higher education institutions. In M. R. Warren & D. Goodman (Eds.), *Lift us up, don't push us out: Voices from the front lines of the educational justice movement* (pp. 118–127). Boston, MA: Beacon Press.

Gist, C. D. (Ed.). (2017). *Portraits of anti-racist alternative routes to teaching in the U.S.* New York: Peter Lang.

Gist, C. D., Bianco, M., & Lynn, M. (2019). Examining grow your own programs across the teacher development continuum: Mining research on teachers of color and nontraditional educator pipelines. *Journal of Teacher Education, 70*(1), 13–25.

Gold, E., Henig, J. R., & Simon, E. (2011, Fall). Calling the shots in public education: Parents, politicians, and educators clash. *Dissent, 58*(4), 34–40.

Gomila, M. A., Pascual, B., & Quincoces, M. (2018). Family-school partnership in the Spanish educational system. *Journal of Education for Teaching, 44*(3), 309–320.

Gonzales, N., Moll, L., & Amanti, C. (2005). *Funds of knowledge: Theorizing practices in households, communities, and classrooms*. Mahwah, NJ: Lawrence Erlbaum.

Goodlad, J. (1994). The National Network for Educational Renewal *Phi Delta Kappan, 75*(8), 632–638.

Goodlad, J. (1998). *Educational renewal: Better teachers, better schools*. San Francisco, CA: Jossey-Bass.

Goodwin, A. L. (2004). Exploring the perspectives of teacher educators of color: What do they bring to teacher education? *Issues in Education, 13*(2), 7–24.

Gorodetsky, M., & Barak, J. (2008). The educational cultural edge: A participative learning environment for co-emergence of personal growth and institutional growth. *Teaching and Teacher Education, 24*(7), 1907–1918.

Grace, G. (2006). Urban education, confronting contradictions: An analysis with special reference to London. *London Review of Education, 4*(2), 115–136.

Graham, R. (1968). The Teacher Corps: One Place to begin. *NASSP Bulletin, 52*(330), 49–61.

Graham, R. (1970). Educational change and the Teacher Corps. *Phi Delta Kappan, 51*(6), 305–310.

Graue, E. (2005). Theorizing and describing preservice teachers' images of families and schooling. *Teachers College Record, 107*(1), 157–185.

Guha, R., Hyler, M. E., & Darling Hammond, L. (2016, September). The teacher residency: An innovative model for preparing teachers. Palo Alto, CA: The Learning Institute. Retrieved from https://learningpolicyinstitute.org/product/teacher-residency.

Guillen, L. (2016). *At the crossroads: Pre-service teachers, community mentors, and the dialectic* [Unpublished doctoral dissertation]. Seattle, WA: College of Education, University of Washington.

Guillen, L., & Zeichner, K. (2018). A university-community partnership in teacher education from the perspectives of community-based teacher educators. *Journal of Teacher Education, 69*(2), 140–153.

Guttman, A. (1999). *Democratic education* (2nd ed.). Princeton, NJ: Princeton University Press.

Haddix, M. (2015). Preparing community-engaged teachers. *Theory into Practice, 54*(1), 63–70.

Haig-Brown, C., & Kawehau Hoskins, T. (2019). Indigenous teacher education in Canada and Autearoa New Zealand. In *Oxford research encyclopedia of education*. Retrieved May 23, 2019, from https://doi.org/10.1093/acrefore/9780190264093.013.746.

Harfitt, G. (2019, July). Community-based experiential learning in teacher education. In G. W. Noblit (Ed.), *Oxford research encyclopedia education*. https://doi.org/10.1093/acrefore/9780190264093.013.986.

Harfitt, G. J., & Chow, J. M. L. (2018). Transforming traditional models of initial teacher education through a mandatory experiential learning programme. *Teaching and Teacher Education, 73*, 120–129.

Hawley, W. B., & Vellanti, J. T. (1970). Trainers of Teachers of Teachers. Washington, DC: ERIC Document Reproduction Service, U.S. Office of Education. Retrieved from https://files.eric.ed.gov/fulltext/ED043593.pdf.

Hayes, S. (1980). The community and teacher education. In H. Prentice, M. Baptiste, & D. Gollnick (Eds.), *Multicultural teacher education* (Vol. 1, pp. 94–108). Washington, DC: American Association of Colleges for Teacher Education.

Heller, R. (2021). The grow your own approach to teacher preparation: An interview with Amaya Garcia. *Phi Delta Kappan, 103*(3), 28–33.

Hodgdon, E. R., & Saunders, R. W. (1951). Using the community in teacher education. *Journal of Teacher Education, 2*(3), 216–218.

Holmes Group. (2007). *The Holmes partnership trilogy.* New York: Peter Lang.

Hong, S. (2011). *A cord of three strands: A new approach to parent engagement.* Cambridge, MA: Harvard Education Press.

Hong, S. (2019). *Natural allies: Hope and possibility in teacher-family partnerships.* Cambridge, MA: Harvard Education Press.

Hyland, N. E., & Meacham, S. (2004). Community knowledge-centered teacher education: A paradigm for socially just educational transformation. In J. L. Kincheloe, S. R. Steinberg, & A. Bursztyn (Eds.), *Building a quality school of urban education* (pp. 113–134). New York: Peter Lang.

Ishimaru, A., Bang, M., Valladres, M., Nolan, C. M., Tavares, H., Rajendran, A., & Chang, K. (2019, July). *Recasting families and communities as co-designers of education in tumultuous times.* Boulder, CO: National Education Policy Center, and Seattle, WA: Family Leadership Design Collaborative.

Ishimaru, A. M. (2020). *Just schools: Building equitable collaborations with families and communities.* New York: Teachers College Press.

Jackson, T. O. (2006). *Learning to teach in freedom schools: Developing practices and identities as educators and activists* [Unpublished doctoral dissertation]. University of Michigan. Retrieved from https://d.lib.msu.edu/etd/38040/datastream/OBJ/View.

Jackson, T. O., & Bryson, B. (2018). Community mapping as a tool for developing culturally relevant pedagogy. *New Educator*, *14*(2), 109–128.

Kirmaci, M. (2019). Reporting educators' experiences regarding family-school interactions with implications for best practices. *School Community Journal*, *29*(2), 129–156.

Kitzmiller, E. (2022). *The roots of inequality: Philadelphia's Germantown high school 1907–2014*. Philadelphia, PA: University of Pennsylvania Press.

Klopfenstein, K. (2005). Beyond test scores: The impact of Black teacher role models on rigorous math taking. *Contemporary Economic Policy*, *23*(3), 416–428.

Koerner, M. E., & Abdul-Tawwab, N. (2006). Using community as a resource for teacher education: A case study. *Equity and Excellence in Education*, *39*(1), 37–46.

Kohli, R. (2021). *Resisting racism and reclaiming education*. Cambridge, MA: Harvard Education Press.

Kohli, R., & Pizarro, M. (2022). The layered toll of racism in teacher education on teacher educators of color. *AERA Open*, *8*(1), 1–12.

Kretchmar, K., & Zeichner, K. (2016). Teacher preparation 3.0: A vision for teacher education to impact social transformation. *Journal of Education for Teaching*, *42*(4), 417–433.

Ladson-Billings, G. (1995). Multicultural teacher education: Issues, policies, and practices. In J. A. Banks & C. M. Banks (Eds.), *Handbook of research on multicultural education* (pp. 747–759). New York: Macmillan.

Ladson-Billings, G. (2021). *Culturally relevant pedagogy: Asking a different question*. New York: Teachers College Press.

Lampert, J. (2021). A community-engaged framework for the preparation of teachers for high poverty communities. *Australian Educational Researcher*, *48*(3), 449–466. Retrieved from https://doi.org/10.1007/s13384-020-00406-8.

Lareau, A. (2000). *Home advantage*. Lanham, MD: Roman & Littlefield.

Lee, R. E. (2018). Breaking down barriers and building bridges: Transformative practices in community-and school-based urban teacher preparation. *Journal of Teacher Education*, *69*(2), 118–126.

Lees, A. (2016). Roles of urban indigenous community members in collaborative field-based teacher preparation. *Journal of Teacher Education, 67*(5), 363–378.

Love, B. L. (2020). *We want to do more than survive: Abolitionist teaching and the pursuit of educational freedom.* Boston, MA: Beacon Press.

Lynch, D., & Smith, R. (2012). Teacher preparation partnerships: An Australian research-based perspective. *Australian Journal of Teacher Education, 37*(11), 132–146.

MacCabe, C., & Yanacek, H. (Eds.). (2018). *Keywords for today: A 21st century vocabulary.* New York: Oxford University Press.

Mahan, J. M. (1993). Teacher education in American Indian communities: Learnings from reservation sources. *Journal of Navajo Education, 11*(1), 13–21.

Maier, A., Daniel, J., Oakes, J., & Lam, L. (2017). *Community schools as an effective school improvement strategy: A review of the evidence.* Palo Alto, CA: Learning Policy Institute. https://learningpolicyinstitute.org/product/community-schools-effective-school-improvement-report.

Mancenido, Z., & Pello, R. (2020). What do we know about how to effectively prepare teachers to engage with families? *School Community Journal, 30*(2), 9–38.

Mapp, K. L., & Bergman, E. (2019). *Dual capacity-building framework for family-school partnerships* (Version 2). Retrieved from www.dualcapacity.org.

Mapp, K. L., & Kuttner, P. J. (2013). *Partners in education: A dual capacity-building framework for family-school partnerships.* Arlington, VA: Southwest Educational Development Laboratory.

Masla, J. A., & Royster, P. M. (1976, February). *Community involvement in teacher education: A study of the models.* Washington, DC: U.S. Department of Health, Education and Welfare. Eric Document Reproduction Service #ED 121 708.

McDiarmid, G. W., & Caprino, K. (2018). *Lessons from the teachers for a new era project.* New York: Routledge.

McDonald, M., Bowman, M., & Brayko, K. (2013). Learning to see students: Opportunities to develop relational practices of teaching through community-based placements in teacher education. *Teachers College Record, 115*(4), 1–35.

Miner, B. J. (2013). *Lessons from the heartland: A turbulent half-century of public education in an iconic American city.* New York: The Free Press.

Mitchell, X. (2008). Traditional vs critical service learning: Engaging the literature to differentiate two models. *Michigan Journal of Community Service Learning, 14*(2), 50–65.

Moon, B. (Ed.). (2016). *Do universities have a role in the education of teachers? An international analysis of policy and practice.* Cambridge: Cambridge University Press.

Mule, L.W. (2010). *Teacher education, diversity, and community engagement in liberal arts colleges.* Lanham, MD: Lexington Books.

Munoz, J. (2020, September). *Culturally responsive teaching: A reflection guide.* Washington, DC: New America. Retrieved from https://files.eric.ed.gov/fulltext/ED609136.pdf.

Murrell, P. (1998). *Like stone soup: The role of the professional development school for the renewal of urban schools.* Washington, DC: American Association of Colleges for Teacher Education.

Murrell, P. (2000). Community teachers: A conceptual framework for preparing exemplary urban teachers. *Journal of Negro Education, 69*(4), 338–348.

Murrell, P. (2001). *The community teacher: A new frame-work for effective urban teaching.* New York: Teachers College Press.

Mustian, A. L., Lee, R. E., Nelson, C., Gamboa-Turner, V., & Roule, L. (2017). Jumping into the deep end: Developing culturally responsive urban teachers through community-immersive partnerships. *Educational Forum, 81*(4), 467–481.

Mustian, A. L., O'Mally, J., Garcia, G., Millan, C., & Zamudio-Mainou, M. L. (2021). Whose voices matter? Intentionality and shared vision. In P. Clark et al. (Eds.), *The power of community-engaged teacher preparation: Voices and visions of hope and healing* (pp. 59–78). New York: Teachers College Press.

Mutton, T., Burn, K., & Thompson, I. (2018). Preparation for family-school partnerships within initial teacher education programmes in England. *Journal of Education for Teaching, 44*(3), 278–295.

Naidoo, L., & Brace, E. (2017). The refugee action support program in Sydney Australia: A bridge between cultures. In L. Hoyt (Ed.), *Regional perspectives on learning by doing: Stories from engaged universities around the world* (pp. 81–102). East Lansing, MI: Michigan State University Press.

Napolitan, K., Traynor, J., Tully, D., Carney, J., Donnelly, S., & Herrenkohl, L. R. (2019). Toward teacher preparation 3.0. *Teachers College Record, 121*(12), 1–41.

National Academies of Sciences, Engineering, and Medicine. (2020). *Changing Expectations for the K-12 Teacher Workforce: Policies, Preservice Education, Professional Development, and the Workplace.*. Washington, DC: The National Academies Press. https://doi.org/10.17226/25603.

National Association for Family, School, and Community Engagement. (2020). *National survey of colleges and universities preparing educators for family engagement*. Retrieved from https://nafsce.org/page/IHEsurvey.

National Center for Educational Statistics. (2021). *The condition of education 2021*. Washington, DC: U.S. Department of Education. Retrieved from https://nces.ed.gov/programs/coe/.

National Center for Education Statistics. (2022). *Digest of education statistics*. Retrieved from https://nces.ed.gov.programs/digest/d21/tables/dt21_204.10.asp.

National Council for the Accreditation of Teacher Education. (2010). *The clinical preparation of teachers: A policy brief*. Washington, DC: Author.

National Study Commission on Undergraduate Education and the Education of Teachers. (1976). *Teacher education in the United States: The responsibility gap*. Lincoln, NE: University of Nebraska Press.

Nguyen, C. D., & Zeichner, K. (2021). Second language teachers learn to teach for social justice through community field experiences. *Language Teaching Research, 25*(4), 656–678.

Noordhoff, K., & Kleinfeld, J. (1993). Preparing teachers for multicultural classrooms. *Teaching and Teacher Education, 9*(1), 27–39.

Oakes, J., Franke, M. L., Quartz, K., & Rogers, J. (2006). Research for high quality urban teaching: Defining it, developing it, and assessing it. *Journal of Teacher Education, 53*(3), 228–235.

Oakes, J., Maier, A., & Daniel, J. (2017, June). *Community schools: An evidence-based strategy for equitable school improvement*. Boulder, CO: National Educational Policy Center, and Palo Alto, CA: Learning Policy Institute. Retrieved from

http://nepc.colorado.edu/publication/equitable-community
-schools.

Olson, P. A. et al. (1975). *What is school-community-based teacher
education and why should administrators be interested in it?*
Lincoln, NE: National Study Commission on Undergraduate
Education and the Education of Teachers. ERIC Document
Reproduction Service # 110-448.

Orland-Barak, L., & Lavrenteva, E. (2019). Global orientations,
local challenges, and promises in initial teacher education. In *The
Oxford research encyclopedia, education.* Retrieved from https://
oxfordre.com/education/view/10.1093/acrefore/9780190264093
.001.0001/acrefore-9780190264093-e-771.

Orr, M., & Rogers, J. (Eds.). (2011). *Public engagement for public
education: Joining forces to revitalize democracy and equalize
schools.* Palo Alto, CA: Stanford University Press.

Pathways Alliance. (2022). Towards a national definition of teacher
residencies. Retrieved from https://www.thepathwaysalliance.org/
teacher-residency-report.

Payne, K. A., & Zeichner, K. (2017). Multiple voices and
participants in teacher education. In D. J. Clandinin & J. Husu
(Eds.), *The Sage handbook of research on teacher education* (pp.
1101–1116). London: Sage Publications Ltd.

Peterson, N., & Gravett, S. (2020). Service learning and teacher
education. In *Oxford research encyclopedia.* Retrieved
from https://oxfordre.com/education/view/10.1093/acrefore
/9780190264093.001.0001/acrefore-9780190264093-e-1002.

Peterson, R. (1999). Survival and justice: Rethinking teacher union
strategy. In R. Peterson & M. Charney (Eds.), *Transforming
teacher unions: Fighting for better schools and social justice* (pp.
11–19). Milwaukee, WI: Rethinking Schools.

Philip, T., Way, W., Garcia, A., Schuler-Brown, S., & Navarro, O.
(2013). When educators attempt to make "community" a part of
classroom learning: The dangers of misappropriating students'
communities into schools. *Teaching and Teacher Education, 34,*
174–183.

Popkewitz, T. (1979). Schools and the symbolic use of community
participation. In C. A. Grant (Ed.), *Community participation in
education* (pp. 202–223). Boston, MA: Allyn & Bacon.

Ramsaroop, S., & Peterson, N. (2020). Building professional
competencies through a service learning gallery walk in primary

teacher education. *Journal of University Teaching and Learning Practice, 17*(4), 1–19.

Reid, C. (2004). *Negotiating racialized identities: Indigenous teacher education in Australia and Canada.* Champaign, IL: Common Ground Publishing.

Reissman, F. (1962). *The culturally deprived child.* New York: Harper and Row.

Richmond, G. (2016). The power of community partnership in the preparation of teachers. *Journal of Teacher Education, 68*(1), 6–8.

Richmond, G. (2017). The power of community partnership in the preparation of teachers. *Journal of Teacher Education, 68*(1), 6–8.

Rogers, B. (2009). "Better" people, better teaching: The vision of the National Teacher Corps, 1965–1968. *History of Education Quarterly, 49*(3), 347–372.

Rogers-Ard, R. (2017). Teach tomorrow Oakland: Combating cultural isolation and opening doors for teachers of color. In C. D. Gist (Ed.), *Portraits of anti-racist alternative routes to teaching in the U.S.* (pp. 17–32). New York: Peter Lang.

Russakoff, D. (2015). *The prize: Who is in charge of America's schools?* Boston, MA: Houghton Mifflin.

Sachs, J. (2001). *The activist teaching profession.* Buckingham: Open University Press.

Saltmarsh, S., Barr, J., & Chapman, A. (2015). Preparing for parents: How Australian teacher education is addressing the question of parent-school engagement. *Asia Pacific Journal of Education, 35*(1), 69–84.

Sarason, S. (1995). *Parental involvement and the political principle.* San Francisco, CA: Jossey Bass.

Scaife, W., & Zygmunt, E. (2021). I am my community: Privileging funds of knowledge and community cultural wealth. In P. Clark, E. Zygmunt, S. Tancock, & K. Howard (Eds.) *The power of community-engaged teacher preparation* (pp. 17–36). New York: Teachers College Press.

Schneider, J., & Berkshire, J. (2020). *A wolf at the schoolhouse door: The dismantling of public education and the future of school.* New York: The New Press.

Schorr, L. B. (1988). *Within our reach: Breaking the cycle of disadvantage.* New York: Doubleday.

Schutz, A. (2006). Home is a prison in the global city: The tragic failure of school-based community engagement strategies. *Review of Educational Research*, 76(4), 691–743.

Sconzert, K., Iazzetto, D., & Purkey, S. (2000). Small-town college to big-city school: Preparing urban teachers from liberal arts colleges. *Teaching and Teacher Education*, 16(4), 465–490.

Seidl, B., & Friend, G. (2002). Leaving authority at the door: Equal-status community-based experiences and the preparation of teachers for diverse classrooms. *Teaching and Teacher Education*, 18(4), 421–433.

Sharkey, J., Olarte, A. C., & Ramierez, L. M. (2016). Developing a deeper understanding of community-based pedagogies with teachers: Learning with and from teachers in Colombia. *Journal of Teacher Education*, 67(4), 306–319.

Shay, M., & Lampert, J. (2020). Community according to whom? An analysis of how indigenous "community" is defined in Australia's through growth to achievement 2018 report on equity in education. *Critical Studies in Education*, 63(1), 47–63.

Skinner, E., Garreton, M. T., & Schultz, B. (Eds.). (2011). *Grow your own teachers: Grassroots change in teacher education*. New York: Teachers College Press.

Sleeter, C. (2001). Preparing teachers for culturally diverse schools: Research and the overwhelming presence of whiteness. *Journal of Teacher Education*, 52(2), 94–106.

Sleeter, C. (2008). Preparing white students for diverse students. In M. Cochran-Smith, S. Feiman-Nemser, & J. McIntyre (Eds.), *Handbook of research on teacher education* (pp. 559–582). New York: Routledge.

Smith, B. O. (1969). Teachers for the real world (3rd ed., pp. 559–582). Washington, DC: American Association of Colleges for Teacher Education, and Mahwah, NJ: Lawrence Erlbaum.

Smith, B. O. (1980). *A design for a school of pedagogy*. Washington, DC: U.S. Department of Education.

Smith, K. (2016). Partnerships in teacher education: Going beyond the rhetoric. *Center for Educational Policy Studies (CEPS Journal)*, 6(3), 17–36.

Smolcic, E., & Katunich, J. (2017). Teachers crossing borders: A review of research into cultural immersion field experiences for teachers. *Teaching and Teacher Education*, 62, 47–59.

Sorenson, L. C., & Ladd, H. (2020). The hidden costs of teacher turnover. *AERA Open*, *6*(1), 1–24.

Souto-Manning, M., & Martell, J. (2019). Toward critically transformative possibilities: Considering tensions and undoing inequities in the spatialization of teacher education. *Teachers College Record*, *121*(6), 1–42.

Stachowski, L. L., & Mahan, J. M. (1998). Cross-cultural field placements: Student teachers learning from schools and communities. *Theory into Practice*, *37*(2), 155–162.

Strauss, V. (2015, September 25). The surprising things Seattle teachers won for students by striking. *Washington Post*. Retrieved August 1, 2020, from https://www.washingtonpost.com/news /answer-sheet/wp/2015/09/25/the-surprising-things-seattle -teachers-won-for-students-by-striking/.

Study Commission on Undergraduate Education and the Education of Teachers. (1976). *Teacher education in the United States: The responsibility gap*. Lincoln, NE: University of Nebraska Press.

Tancock, S., Zygmunt, E., Clark, P., Clausen, J., & Mucherah, W. (2017). Fostering culturally relevant children's literature knowledge with a community-engaged literacy event. *Reading Professor*, *39*(1), 20–26.

Thomas, M. A. M., Rauschenberger, E., & Crawford-Garrett, K. (2022). *Examining teach for all*. London: Routledge.

Thompson, I., Willemse, M., Mutton, T., Burn, K., & deBruine, E. (Eds.). (2018). Teacher education and family-school partnerships in different contexts: A cross country analysis of national teacher education frameworks across a range of European countries. *Journal of Education for Teaching*, *44*(3), 258–277.

Tuck, E. (2009). Suspending damage: A letter to communities. *Harvard Educational Review*, *79*(3), 409–427.

Van Winkle, K. (2017). Grow your own (GYO) Illinois: Creating teachers and community leaders. In C. Gist (Ed.), *Portraits of anti-racist alternative routes to teaching in the U.S.* (pp. 77–92). New York: Peter Lang.

Villegas, A. M., & Irvine, J. J. (2010). Diversifying the teaching force: An examination of the major arguments. *Urban Review*, *42*(3), 175–192.

Villegas, A. M., & Lucas, T. (2002). *Educating culturally responsive teachers: A coherent approach*. Albany, NY: SUNY Press.

Waite, S., Mentor, M., & Bristol, T. J. (2018). Growing our own: Reflections on developing a pipeline for male educators of color. *Journal of the Center for Policy Analysis and Research*, *1*(1), 148–166.

Waller, W. (1932). *The sociology of teaching*. New York: John Wiley & Sons.

Warren, M. (2011). The school-community organizing model and the origins of grow your own teachers. In E. A. Skinner, M. T. Garreton, & B. Schultz (Eds.), *Grow your own teachers: Grassroots change in teacher education* (pp. 34–48). New York: Teachers College Press.

Warren, M. R., & Goodman, D. (Eds.). (2018). *Lift me up, don't push me out: Voices from the front lines of the education justice movement*. Boston, MA: Beacon.

Watson, V. (2012). *Learning to liberate: Community-based solutions to the crisis in urban education*. New York: Routledge.

Weiss, H. B., Lopez, E., & Caspe, M. (2018, October). *Joining together to create a bold vision for next generation family engagement: Engaging families to transform education*. New York: Carnegie Corporation of New York. Retrieved from https://globalfrp.org/content/download/419/3823/file/GFRP_Family%20Engagement%20Carnegie%20Report.pdf.

Weiss, H. B., Lopez, M. E., & Rosenberg, H. (2010). *Beyond random acts: Family, school, and community engagement as an integral part of school reform*. Washington, DC: U.S. Department of Education. Retrieved December 1, 2021, from https://sedl.org/connections/engagement_forum/beyond_random_acts.pdf.

Whitinuip, P., Rodriguez de Francem, M., & Mclvor, O. (Eds.). (2018) *Promising practices in Indigenous teacher education*. Singapore: Springer.

Will, M. (2019, May 14). 65 years after Brown v. board: Where are all the Black educators? *Education Week*. Retrieved August 11, 2021, from https://www.edweek.org/policy-politics/65-years-after-brown-v-board-where-are-all-the-black-educators/2019/05.

Williams, R. (1976). *Keywords: A vocabulary of culture and society*. Oxford: Oxford University Press.

Yosso, T. J. (2005). Whose culture has capital? A critical race theory discussion of community cultural wealth. *Race and Education*, *8*(1), 69–91.

Zeichner, K. (2010). Rethinking the connections between campus courses and field experiences in college and university-based teacher education. *Journal of Teacher Education*, 89(11), 89–99.

Zeichner, K. (2019a). Preparing teachers as democratic professionals. *Action in Teacher Education*, 42(1), 38–48.

Zeichner, K. (2019b). Moving beyond asset, equity, and justice oriented teacher education. *Teachers College Record*, 12(6), 1–5.

Zeichner, K. (2021). Critical unresolved and understudied issues in clinical teacher education. *Peabody Journal of Education*, 96(1), 1–7.

Zeichner, K. (2022). Interview with Ken Zeichner: Current challenges and future possibilities for teacher education. *Asia-Pacific Journal of Teacher Education*, 50(2), 130–143.

Zeichner, K., Bowman, M., Guillen, L., & Napolitan, K. (2016). Engaging and working in solidarity with local communities in preparing the teachers of their children. *Journal of Teacher Education*, 67(4), 277–290.

Zeichner, K., & Melnick, S. (1996a). The role of community field experiences in preparing teachers for cultural diversity. In K. Zeichner, S. Melnick, & M. L. Gomez (Eds.), *Currents of reform in preservice teacher education* (pp. 176–198). New York: Teachers College Press.

Zeichner, K., & Melnick, S. (1996b). Community field experiences and teacher preparation for diversity: Case study. In D. J. McIntryre & W. M. Bird (Eds.), *Preparing tomorrow's teachers: The field experience* (pp. 41–61). Thousand Oaks, CA: Corwin Press.

Zeichner, K., Payne, K., & Brayko, K. (2015). Democratizing teacher education. *Journal of Teacher Education*, 66(2), 122–135.

Zygmunt, E., & Cipollone, K. (2018). A pedagogy of promise: Critical service learning as praxis in community-engaged, culturally responsive teacher preparation. In M. Dowell & T. Meidl (Eds.), *Service learning initiatives in teacher education programs* (pp. 333–354). Hershey, PA: IGI Global.

Zygmunt, E., Cipollone, K., Clark, P., & Tancock, S. (2018, September). Community-engaged teacher preparation. In G. W. Noblit (Ed.), *Oxford research encyclopedia education*. https://doi.org/10.1093/acrefore/9780190264093.013.476

Zygmunt, E., Cipollone, S., Tancock, S., Clausem, J., Clark, P., & Mucherah, W. (2018). Loving out loud: Community mentors, teacher candidates, and transformational learning through a pedagogy of care and connection. *Journal of Teacher Education*, 69(2), 127–139.

Zygmunt, E., & Clark, P. (2015). *Transforming teacher education for social justice*. New York: Teachers College Press.

INDEX

AACTE; *see* American
Association for
Colleges of Teacher
Education (AACTE)
AAQEP; *see* Association for
Advancing Quality in
Educator Preparation
(AAQEP)
accreditation agencies 39–40
African American Ethnic
Academy 59–62
curriculum 60
Harambee time 60
Kwanzaa celebration 60
teachers 61
volunteers 61–2
African Americans
community 54
ethnic academy 59–62
families xiv
rights xiv
students 54
Alanko, A. 38
The Alliance for Community
Engaged Teacher
Preparation, Ball
State 36
American Association
for Colleges of
Teacher Education
(AACTE) 36

American Association of
Teachers Colleges 21
American Indian Studies
program faculty 55
Archibald, J. 69
Association for Advancing
Quality in Educator
Preparation
(AAQEP) 40

Ball State 36, 45, 63
school 45
university 54
Barajas-Lopez, F. 2
Barak, J. 97–8
Benjamin Banneker school 54
BIPOC students 2–3, 53, 76
BIPOC teachers 43, 76
Black Prisoners Caucus 46
Blair, L. 22
Boyle-Baise, Marilynn 54
Bryk, A. 8
Burn, K. 37

CAEP; *see* Council for the
Accreditation of
Educator Programs
(CAEP)
Cardozo Project, Urban
Teaching 25
Carnegie Corporation 32

Caspe, M.   12, 40
Chicago Teacher Education
        Pipeline, United States
        35, 45, 51, 78–9
Civil Rights Act   xiv
class segregation   22
communities   xiii, xviii
    civil rights struggles   3
    concept   xiii
    and families, involving
        versus engaging in
        schools   10–13
    members   xiii, 44–5
    nondominant   xviii, 2
    in TPPs   xix, 44–56
    United States   3, 19–40
communities in teacher
        education   xiii, xix,
        19–100
    approach   xiii, xvii, 16,
        19–40, 87–8
    in English-speaking
        countries   20
    literature on   20, 22
    attempts/examples   33–6
    clinical experiences in   21–3,
        26, 33, 36
    design principles for working
        with   74–94
        community-teacher
            education partnerships
            94
        design characteristics
            84–5
        power/trust/reciprocity in
            relationships   85–91
    teacher candidate
        experiences in
        communities   91–4
    teacher educators   74–84
    experiences   21–6

global trends in   36–40
in higher education
        institutions   26
homegrown teachers
        in nondominant
        communities   66–9
lack of attention to   36–7
multicultural movement in
        23
nondominant communities
        roles   32–3
participation in TPPs   9–10,
        25, 28, 30–2, 42–56
    engagement   50–1
    how   44–5
    involvement   48–50
    knowledge-power
        relationships in   47–9
    who   45–7
    working in solidarity
        52–6
partnerships   13, 16, 32–40
programs   xix–xx, 20–40
    accreditation agencies for
        39–40
    aspects of   44–5
    Cardozo Project   25
    communities in   xix,
        21–40
    engagement in   50–1
    GYO programs   xx, 45,
        47, 67–8, 82
    indigenous   xx, 20, 45,
        68–9
    involvement   48–50
    working in solidarity
        52–6
public schools for   21
responsibility gap in   29–31
social-justice-oriented
        approach   24–8

National Institute for Advanced Study in Teaching Disadvantaged Youth (1976) report   27–8
Study Commission on Undergraduate Education and Teacher Education report 29–33
Teacher Corps (1965–81) 24–7
system supports for   94–9
teacher candidates experiences   57–66
  activities and settings in 57–8
  length/depth of   57
  in private community-based school   59–62
  and programs   62–5
  in public community school   59
  schools as settings for 58
  stance toward communities   65–7
  to teach in culturally responsive and sustaining ways 14–17
  typology   42
  to work with families/communities   36–40
communities involvement   xix, 21–40, 44–5
community cultural wealth 12
community elites   26
community-engaged teacher educators   74

Community-Engaged Teacher Preparation, Ball State   36
community engagement 11–12, 48, 50–1
Cook, B.   31
Council for Chief State School Officers Network for Transforming Educator Preparation   32
Council for the Accreditation of Educator Programs (CAEP)   39–40
CRS teachers   85–6, 91
CSP; see culturally sustaining pedagogy (CSP)
cultural dexterity   15
culturally sustaining pedagogy (CSP)   15–16
curriculum   6, 13–14, 22, 38, 56, 60–1, 71, 76, 80

deBruine, E.   37
democratic professionalism 4–5
design principles, communities in teacher education 74–94
  community-teacher education partnerships   94
  design characteristics   84–5
  power/trust/reciprocity in relationships   85–91
  teacher candidate experiences in communities 91–4
  teacher educators   74–84
"Dual Capacity-Building Framework for Family-School Partnerships, A" 12–13

educational reform 17
elementary teacher education
        program 49–50
Erickson, O. 22
expertise 10

faculty 28–30, 35–6, 48–9, 54–5,
        57, 62, 78–83, 86–7
families
    and communities/schools,
        disconnect and distrust
        between 6–10
    and educators, relationships
        between 10–13
    involving *versus* engaging in
        schools 10–13
    members 4, 44–5
    teacher education programs,
        participation in 44–5
    in teacher preparation
        programs xix, 14–17,
        25–6
family-community-school
        partnerships 36–40
    in Australia 37–8
    in Europe 37
    in Finland 38
    in teacher education
        programs 19–40
    in United States 19–36
Family Leadership Design
        Collaborative 88
Finklea, T. 40
First Nations Educational
        Council 69
Fratney School 59
funds/funding 2, 4, 7, 12–13,
        15, 26, 28–30, 32,
        34–5, 44, 52, 54, 69,
        73, 83, 95–100

Garcia, A. 45
Gorodetsky, M. 97–8
Grow Your Own (GYO)
        programs xx, 45, 47,
        67–8, 82
Guillen, L. 92

Haddix, Marcelle 63–4, 77–8,
        91
Harambee time 60
Hayes, S. 23
Holmes Group Partnership 32
homegrown teachers
        preparation 66–9
home-school relations 9
Hyland, N. E. 31

Indigenous Roots Teacher
        Education Program
        (ROOTS) in
        Nebraska 35, 69
The Indigenous Teacher
        Education Program,
        British Columbia,
        Canada 35, 69
indigenous teacher education
        programs xx, 20, 45,
        68–9
indigenous teachers 35, 68–9
Ishimaru, A. M. 2

Katunich, J. 13
knowledge 10, 12
knowledge-power relationships
        47–9
Kothari, U. 31
Kuttner, P. J. 12–13
Kwanzaa celebration 60

La Escuela Fratney 59

La Trobe University, Australia
46–7
Lavrenteva, E. 38
Lees, A. 93, 98
LGBGT issues 3
Logan Square neighborhood
association
(LSNA) 47, 68
Lopez, E. 12
LSNA; *see* Logan Square
neighborhood
association (LSNA)

Mapp, K. L. 12–13
Meacham, S. 31
Monaco, M. 40
multicultural movement in
teacher education 23
Munoz, J. 15
Murrell, Peter 100
Mutton, T. 37

National Association for
Family, School,
and Community
Engagement
(NAFSCE) 36
National Institute for Advanced
Study in Teaching
Disadvantaged Youth
(1976) report 27–8
National Network for
Educational
Renewal 32
Native Education Certificate
program 56
Navajo Nation Project, Indiana
University 34, 62
Navarro, O. 45
NDEA task force 27–9

goals 27
local communities, role
for 28
nondominant communities
xviii, 2, 24
CRS teaching in 86
definition 2
education to 7
exploitation of 86
families/communities/schools,
disconnect and distrust
between 6–10
homegrown teachers
preparation in
66–9
members 4, 44–5
public schools 8
school-community
connections in
xviii–xix
systemic problems in 5
teacher preparation
programs, role
in 32–3
teachers in 6–8
teaching in 6
in United States 4–5
nondominant families xviii
definition 2
participation with schools 9

Obama, Barack 61
Orland-Barak, L. 38

parent-teacher work 10–13
Peace Corps volunteers 25
Peterson, R. 53
Philip, T. 45
Popkewitz, T. 31
poverty 2, 22

Pre-service Family Engagement Consortium 36
public schools
    students 2–3, 22
    teacher xiii
    Teacher Corps projects for 24–7

racism 3, 22
relational agency 104 n.3
Rethinking Schools 59

Sachs, J. 4
Schneider, B. 8
schools
    class segregation in 22
    community cultural practices, absence of 7
    improvement efforts in 8–9
    involving *versus* engaging families/communities in 10–13
    racial segregation in 22
Schools Within the Context of Community program, United States 35–6
school-university-based teacher education programs 30
school-university partnerships 33, 38–9
Schuler-Brown, S. 45
Seattle Teacher Residency Program 46
service learning experiences 81–2
Smith, B. O. 28
Smolcic, E. 13
social justice teacher unionism 52–4

social mobility 7
students
    communities 22–3
    public school 22
Study Commission on Undergraduate Education and Teacher Education report 29–33
    1980s–Today 32–3
    US teacher education, responsibility gap 29–31

TC; *see* Teacher Corps (TC)
teacher candidates, community experiences for 57–66, 91–4
    activities and settings 57–8
    length/depth 57
    in private community-based school 59–62
    and programs 62–5
    in public community school 59
    schools as settings for 58
    service learning experiences 81–2
    stance toward communities 65–7
teacher certification 39
Teacher Corps (TC) xvi, 24–7, 44
    community participation in 25–7
    goals 24–5
    interns xvi, 25
    projects xvi, 25
    for teacher preparation in United States 24–7

tripartite model of
preparation 25
teacher education
accreditation agencies
for 39–40
brief attempts/long long-
lasting examples
33–6
community-engaged
approach in xiii, xvii,
xix, 16, 19–40, 87–8
aspects of 44–5
in English-speaking
countries 20
literature on 20, 22
who 45–7
global trends in 36–40
hybrid/third spaces for 98
multicultural movement
in 23
programs xix–xx, 20
accreditation agencies
for 39–40
Cardozo Project 25
communities engagement
in 50–1
communities
involvement xix,
21–40, 44–5, 48–50
communities working in
solidarity 52–6
elementary 49–50
families in 44–5
GYO programs xx, 45,
47, 67–8, 82
indigenous xx, 20, 45,
68–9
public schools for 21
responsibility gap in 29–31
school-university-based 30

social-justice-oriented
approach in 24–8
National Institute
for Advanced
Study in Teaching
Disadvantaged Youth
(1976) report 27–8
Study Commission
on Undergraduate
Education and Teacher
Education report
29–33
Teacher Corps (1965-
81) 24–7
system supports for
community
partnerships in 94–9
work of xiii
for work with families/
communities 36–40
teacher educators xiii, xvi–xvii,
74–84
community-engaged 74–84
and community
participants 86
teacher preparation programs
(TPPs) xix–xx,
19–100
communities in xix, 19–72
engagement 50–1
how 44–5
involvement 48–50
knowledge-power
relationships in 47–9
who 45–7
working in solidarity
52–6
in higher education
institutions 26
lack of attention to 36–7

nondominant communities
  role in 32–3
Teacher Corps 24–7
to teach in culturally
  responsive and
  sustaining ways
  14–17
to work with families/
  communities 36–40
teacher residency
  programs 104 n.4
"Teachers for the Real World"
  (Smith) 27
Teach for All program 6
Thompson, I. 37
TPPs; *see* teacher preparation
  programs (TPPs)
Trainer of Teacher Trainers
  program 44
Tubman, Harriet 60

United States 2
  BIPOC students 2–3
  communities across 3
  nondominant communities
    in 4–5
  poverty in 2–3

public schools students 2–3
  teacher education 19–100
University of Massachusetts-
  Boston 80
University of Washington
  45–6, 55–6, 63–4, 92
university teacher
  educators 31, 87
Urban Education Program,
  Associated Colleges of
  the Midwest 34, 62
urban teachers 80
US Department of Education
  Teacher Quality
  Partnership
  Grants 95

Voting Rights Act xiv

W. K. Kellogg Foundation 95
Warren, M. 67
Way, W. 45
Weiss, H. B. 12
Willemse, M. 37
Williams, R. 2

Zeichner, K. 92

www.ingramcontent.com/pod-product-compliance
Ingram Content Group UK Ltd.
Pitfield, Milton Keynes, MK11 3LW, UK
UKHW020715280225
455688UK00012B/369